THE
LITURGICAL
MINISTRY
SERIES

GUIDE FOR SERVERS

Corinna Laughlin
Robert D. Shadduck
Paul Turner
D. Todd Williamson

LTP

LITURGY
TRAINING
PUBLICATIONS

In accordance with c. 827, permission to publish is granted on May 19, 2009, by the Very Reverend John F. Canary, Vicar General of the Archdiocese of Chicago. Permission to publish is an official declaration of ecclesiastical authority that the material is free from doctrinal and moral error.

The prayers on pages 16, 17, 18, 19, 20, 21, 22, 24, 25, and 26 were written by Paul Turner.

THE LITURGICAL MINISTRY SERIES: GUIDE FOR SERVERS © 2009 Archdiocese of Chicago: Liturgy Training Publications, 3949 South Racine Avenue, Chicago IL 60609; 1-800-933-1800, fax 1-800-933-7094, e-mail orders@ltp.org. All rights reserved. See our Web site at www.LTP.org.

The cover photo and photos on pages vi, 1, 50, 52, 54, and 72 © John Zich. The photo on page 49 © Sandy Bertog. The photo on page 70 © Yvette M. Dostatni.

The images on pages 36 and 80 were designed by M. Urgo.

Printed in the United States of America.

Library of Congress Control Number: 2009927078

ISBN 978-1-56854-803-6

ELSER

Psalm 135:1b–3

Praise the name of the LORD!
Praise, you servants of the LORD,
Who stand in the house of the LORD,
in the courts of the house of our God!
Praise the LORD; the LORD is good!
Sing to God's name; it is gracious!

I should memorize

Table of Contents

Preface   vii

Welcome   1

Theology and History of the Server   4

Spirituality and Formation of the Server   15

Serving the Liturgy   30

Frequently Asked Questions   78

Resources   84

Glossary   88

Preface

I have given you a model to follow, so that as I have done for you, you should also do.

—*John 13:15*

Jesus looked down at their feet and furrowed his brow. This would never do. How could he enjoy the last meal of his life when the disciples didn't even clean up before coming in?

Jesus had a thing about manners at meals. Oh, he ate and drank with tax collectors and sinners, and he did it with enough gusto to offend his enemies.[1] But usually Jesus expected customs to be observed and order to be maintained. Before the miracle of the loaves he specified that the crowd should break into groups of fifty.[2] At a Pharisee's house he scolded the dinner guests jockeying for the best places at the table.[3] He corrected a host who invited friends and not the poor, the crippled, the lame, and the blind.[4] When he was a guest at the home of another Pharisee he expected a kiss in welcome, oil for his head, and water for his feet.[5] He got none of it. The one time he skipped the pre-meal washing ritual, he wanted to expose the impure intents of the Pharisees.[6]

Table manners also show up in the parables of Jesus. He told about people foolishly declining a dinner invitation from the king, who then berated one of the guests because he showed up wearing the wrong clothes.[7] Another parable depicts a jealous man who refuses to join the party when his prodigal younger brother returns home from an indulgent fling.[8] Another parable criticizes five women who brought so little oil that they missed their chance to eat at the wedding banquet when they left to restock the provisions for their lamps.[9] In another parable a rich man sinfully gives table scraps to dogs, but not to a human beggar.[10]

Jesus loved to eat, and he enjoyed the company of friends and opponents. But he had some expectations of hosts and guests alike. He never shook those expectations, not even on the night before he died.

When the disciples showed up for the meal, they probably had no idea that Jesus was about to unveil Eucharist for them. They probably entered and sat down in their usual spirit of camaraderie. Jesus decided to set a more proper tone right away.

He took off his clothing and tied a large towel around his waist. He tipped a vase of water into a basin and scooted across the floor to the sandaled toes of the nearest disciple. He stuck each disciples' feet into the basin and scrubbed them with the towel. Then he went to the next disciple. And to the next. The water muddied. The towel turned dark.

Jesus came to Simon Peter, who couldn't believe what he was seeing. "Master, are you going to wash my feet?"[11] Jesus rolled his eyes and sighed, probably thinking, "Isn't it obvious?" But what he said was more polite: "What I am doing, you do not understand now, but you will understand later."[12]

It was polite, but it reminded Peter how stupid he sometimes felt in the presence of his master. "He keeps telling me I don't understand," Peter thought. Then he got an idea. He decided Jesus was testing him. Here was his chance to make an impression, to show he wasn't as ignorant as Jesus thought he was. Bravely, confidently, Peter uttered a command: "You will never wash my feet,"[13] and winked.

Wrong. This was not the response Jesus wanted. Jesus sighed and explained, "Unless I wash you, you will have no inheritance with me."[14]

"Now I get it," Peter thought. He had another idea. Obviously he had taken the wrong extreme. "Master, then not only my feet, but my hands and head as well."[15] Peter grinned.

Wrong again. Not the response Jesus wanted, either. Jesus just shook his head and lifted Peter's ankle.

When Jesus finished washing the feet of all the disciples, he put on his clothes and joined them at the table. It was time to start the lecture. "Do you realize what I have done for you?"[16] Of course, they didn't.

Jesus continued, "You call me 'teacher' and 'master,' and rightly so, for indeed I am."[17] Peter felt relieved that at least they got that much right. Now Jesus taught as the master he was: "If I, therefore, the master and teacher, have washed your feet, you ought to wash one another's feet. I have given you a model to follow, so that as I have done for you, you should also do."[18]

Before Jesus ate and drank for the last time with his friends, he taught them a final lesson about service. It wasn't just manners after all. It wasn't just about conventional behavior. It was about hospitality and humility. You don't eat and drink unless you also serve.

In the end, Jesus wasn't concerned about whose feet were clean. He cared about who cleaned feet. Mass loses some of its splendor if it is not celebrated by people who also serve. Those who set an example, right up front in the sanctuary, are the people we call by a title that would make Jesus nod in approval: they are servers.

Paul Turner

NOTES

1. See Matthew 9:10–13; 11:19.

2. See Luke 9:14.

3. See Luke 14:7–11.

4. See Luke 14:12–14.

5. See Luke 7:44–46.

6. See Luke 11:37–40.

7. See Matthew 22:1–14.

8. See Luke 15:25–32.

9. See Matthew 25:1–13.

10. See Luke 16:19–31.

11. John 13:6.

12. John 13:7.

13. John 13:8.

14. Ibid.

15. John 13:9.

16. John 13:12.

17. John 13:13.

18. John 13:14–15.

Welcome

You are volunteering as a server at church. You light candles, hold the books, handle the vessels, and arrange the cloths. You help the other ministers focus on their work by simplifying their motions and eliminating distractions. You help the entire community celebrate Eucharist by your humble service.

Your actions may seem routine, but everyone depends on you to do them without flash. When you serve well, no one notices you. People only notice when things go awry. The greatest compliment they give you is to ignore that you are there.

Serving Mass has long been an opportunity for children. It teaches them about Mass and involves them right at the altar. Children who start at a young age can spend a lifetime serving the Church in many other ways.

Still, the Church relies on the assistance of adult servers. Whether in parishes, convents, monasteries, or chapels, adults serve Mass. They join in the prayer, and they assure the smooth execution of the liturgy.

The Church relies on the assistance of adult servers.

About this Book

You may be new to serving. Or you may already know your job well. This book will affirm you and help you understand even more about the parts of Mass and the service you give. You will find tips for serving better and suggestions to deepen your prayer life. You will also reflect on the service you give outside of Mass, and see how the different parts of your life fit together.

Disciples of Jesus are called to worship and to serve, to eat, to drink—and to wash feet. You do it all, especially when you act as a server at Mass.

About the Authors

This book is the collaborative work of four authors. Paul Turner wrote the first sections of the book, "Preface," "Welcome," "Theology and History of the Sacristan," and "Spirituality and Formation of the Sacristan." He is the pastor of St. Munchin parish in Cameron, Missouri, and its mission, St. Aloysius in Maysville. A priest of the diocese of Kansas City–St. Joseph, he holds a doctorate in sacred theology from Sant' Anselmo in Rome. He is the author of many pastoral resources about sacraments and the liturgy.

"Serving the Liturgy," "Frequently asked Questions," "Resources," and the "Glossary" were written by Corinna Laughlin, Robert D. Shadduck, and D. Todd Williamson.

Corinna Laughlin is the director of liturgy for St. James Cathedral in Seattle. She is also a member of the Liturgical Commission of the Archdiocese of Seattle. She has written articles for *Pastoral Liturgy*® and *Today's Liturgy*. Corinna is the author of LTP's *The Liturgical Ministry Series: Guide for Sacristans; Sourcebook for Sundays, Seasons, and Weekdays: The Almanac for Pastoral Liturgy 2009*; and she is the coauthor of *Daily Prayer 2010* with Ward Johnson. She holds a doctorate in English language and literature from the University of Washington and a bachelor's degree in English from Mount Holyoke College. Visit the Web site of St. James Cathedral at www.stjames-cathedral.org.

Robert D. Shadduck is currently the ministry head for a large altar server program at Padre Serra Parish in Camarillo, California. He holds a Certificate of Director of Liturgy from the Archdiocese of Los Angeles. He has served as master of ceremonies for several bishops and has worked with the RCIA process in the capacity of director of rites and catechist. Robert Shadduck received his bachelor's and master's degrees from Loyola University of Los Angeles.

D. Todd Williamson is the director of the Office for Divine Worship of the Archdiocese of Chicago. He is a noted speaker and liturgist whose ministerial experience includes teaching, and campus and parish pastoral ministry. Todd earned his Master in Theological Studies, with a concentration in liturgy, from Chicago's Catholic Theological Union. He is coauthor of *Let the Mystery Lead You! Bringing Liturgy and Catechesis Together* (Twenty-third Publications), the author of *Sourcebook for Sundays and Seasons:*

A Parish Almanac for 2007 and 2008, and has written articles for *Catechumenate, Pastoral Liturgy* ®, *Rite,* and RTJ (*Religion Teachers Journal*). The Web site for the Office for Divine Worship is www.ODW.org.

Questions for Discussion and Reflection

1. Why have you agreed to help as a server at your church?

_____

_____

_____

_____

2. What do you hope to gain in your understanding of the theology and function of the ministry through this book?

_____

_____

_____

_____

Theology and History of the Server

Understanding Serving

The server is both a member of the assembly and a minister in the sanctuary. With a foot in both worlds, the server has an unusual perspective when participating at Mass. To help you appreciate the work you do, look first at the big picture: what we do at Mass, and why we serve at all.

Eucharist

The word *Eucharist* means "thanksgiving." It comes from a Greek word. To this day, when modern Greeks say, "Thank you," they say *"Eucharisto."* It is one of the most used words in the language.

> ✠ [This sacrament is called] Eucharist, because it is an action of thanksgiving to God. The Greek words *eucharistein* (cf. Lk 22:19; 1 Cor 11:24) and *eulogein* (cf. Mt 26:26; Mk 14:22) recall the Jewish blessings that proclaim— especially during a meal—God's works: creation, redemption, and sanctification.
>
> —*Catechism of the Catholic Church (CCC), 1328*

Mass is an act of thanksgiving. Through it we call to mind the great deeds God has done for us, and we express our gratitude for them. We do this especially in the prayers.

Almost all the prayers at Mass begin with some reason to give God thanks. One example of this structure is the Collect—the Opening Prayer, the one the priest offers just before everyone sits down to hear the readings. The Collect usually calls upon God by some title, then it states something wonderful that God has done, then it makes a petition, and it concludes with a formula of praise through Christ in the Holy Spirit—to which everyone answers, "Amen."

The Collect may give thanks to God for various reasons: the presence of Christ, his future coming, the mercy of forgiveness, or the power and wisdom of God. On special days of the year we thank God for the birth of Jesus, for his manifestation to the Magi, his baptism in the Jordan, his triumph over temptation, his cross, his Resurrection, his Ascension, and the coming of the Holy Spirit. We do not just commemorate these events, we thank God for them.

The same point is made in other prayers. The preface for the Eucharistic Prayer, the Prayer over the Offerings, and the Prayer after Communion may all express reasons to give thanks. Even in the Lord's Prayer, we acknowledge that God is our Father in heaven whose name deserves reverence, whose kingdom comes, and whose good will should be done. We give thanks for all of that before we ask for bread, forgiveness, and preservation from evil.

You structure requests like this in your own life. If you need a favor from someone, you probably start by acknowledging how good he (or she) is, how generously he has acted in the past, and how he inspires others. Once you have given praise, once you have said thanks for who that person is and what that person has done, *then* you ask your favor. The favor goes farther if you have first said thank you.

The reason we give so much thanks to God is the size of our request. We want the Holy Spirit to transform bread and wine into the body and blood of Christ, and to transform us who share this Holy Communion into a more unified and peaceful whole.

Some people might say they come to Mass primarily to receive Holy Communion. And this is important. We receive the Body and Blood of Christ, which nourishes us in the week ahead. Other people might say they come to Mass primarily to ask for God's help in their struggles. This is also important; God is anxious to hear our prayers and to respond to our needs.

But by the very name *Eucharist* we learn we have another responsibility at Mass: to give God thanks and praise. We come not just to get something, and not just to ask for something. We come to say something. We say thank you. Our words of thanks are linked to our request for the Holy Spirit, but God deserves our thanks even without a petition. God deserves our praise.

The word *Mass* means "sending." It comes from the Latin words that conclude the service, "*Ite, missa est.*" It has been translated many ways, such as "Go, the Mass is ended." Or, more freely, "Go in peace to love and serve the Lord." It's not too much of a stretch to translate it this way: "Go, you have been sent."

We call this part of Mass the dismissal, but it is not just a "sending from." It is a "sending to." We are not just ending our time of prayer together. We are beginning our time of service. The very word *Mass* implies that something follows. We do not celebrate without also being sent. We spend the Mass praying for transformation, and we spend the week putting our refreshed selves to work for the sake of the reign of God.

> ✠ [This sacrament is called] *Holy Mass* (*Missa*), because the liturgy in which the mystery of salvation is accomplished concludes with the sending forth (*missio*) of the faithful, so that they may fulfill God's will in their daily lives.
> —CCC, 1332

Sunday, the Lord's Day

Sunday is the day we set aside for this worship. It is the Lord's Day, the day on which we celebrate the rising of Christ. Because he rose from the dead on the first day of the week, we gather on that day to give thanks.

When we celebrate Eucharist on Sunday, we affirm two great beliefs: that Jesus Christ is risen from the dead, and that he is truly present in the bread and wine consecrated at Mass. These beliefs go together. Jesus Christ is present in Eucharist because he is risen. He rose in order to be present with us more fully, freed from the constraints of time and place.

Still, we gather at a specific time and a particular place for Eucharist. Sunday Mass may also take place on Saturday night. The Catholic Church recognizes the ancient tradition of starting the day on the evening before. This, too, testifies to our faith. We face the coming darkness with the light of belief. As surely as the sun will rise, so we believe that we shall rise after the darkness of death. When we gather on Saturday evening, we confront the gathering darkness with the faith of Easter.

A Place for Worship

The place for our Eucharist is a church set aside for this purpose. This building is where the faithful gather. We fill it with our faith. It resounds with our conviction. It takes its personality from those who gather. When a single building is used from one generation to the next, it becomes a storehouse of the faith of ages past. It is infused with the spirit of our ancestors and enlivened by the communion of saints in heaven and on earth.

You don't need a building to worship God. You may worship at home. You may thank God for creation by watching the sun rising over the hill, or gathering its reddish rays distended across the waters at the end of the day. But a church is special. It is a designated building where our faith lives. It is our house, and it is God's house.

The People of God as Church

The people who gather there on Sunday morning are the Church. The word *church* ultimately derives from a Greek word meaning "the house of the Lord,"[1] but we use it to translate a different Greek word, "*ekklesia*," which refers to the gathering of the faithful. So our word *church* means both the building and the people. It comes from a word meaning "the building," but it refers to a word meaning "the people."

WE GATHER: We each hold individual faith in our hearts, but we are connected to one another. When we gather, we form something larger than ourselves. We may pray and serve privately, but we do many actions at Mass together. We arrive together. We sing together. We assume postures together. We make the responses together. We listen to God's word together. We observe the silences together. We pray together in silence while the priest speaks words to God. We lift our hearts and give thanks together. We share Holy Communion together. And we are dismissed together. Together we go forth from Mass as one body on a mission.

WE SERVE: Everyone has the responsibility to worship, and everyone has the responsibility to serve. Most people serve without even thinking about it. Parents care for their children. Students watch out for their friends. Workers make the world a better place.

Some service, though, is freely chosen with a special purpose in mind. You help at a food pantry. You deliver meals to the homebound. You babysit the neighbor's kids. You contribute to charities. You visit the hospitalized. Such service requires a decision on your part. You choose it in order to help out, and you immediately feel the rewards.

Service makes us think less of ourselves and more of the common good. "The common good is always oriented towards the progress of persons: 'The order of things must be subordinate to the order of persons, and not the other way around' [*Gaudium et Spes*, 26 §3]. This order is founded on truth, built up in justice, and animated by love."[2] Without service, we care only about our own income and comfort. Without service, we cannot enter meaningful relationships with other people. Without service, we can never know the happiness we were created to experience.

> ✚ The common good is always oriented towards the progress of persons.
>
> —*CCC, 1912*

Our service is directed away from ourselves and toward two ends: toward God and toward others. Outwardly, it appears that our service is toward other people. It gives them a lift when they are down. It gives them hope for tomorrow. It makes the world a more pleasant place to live.

Inwardly, though, our service is toward God. By helping our neighbor we show our love for God. It is one thing to say you love God, you thank God, and you praise God. But it is another thing to show it. You know this from your primary relationships. You may think you love someone, you may even say you love someone, but if you never show it by your sacrifice, your words ring hollow. You probably love being loved more than you love loving. When you show your love for your neighbor, you show your love for God.

Everyone is expected to serve, and you are fulfilling this expectation in a specific way: as a server at Mass. No matter what age you are, your service at Mass helps your neighbor and expresses your love for God.

As a server, you help the ministers and the people. You hold a candle to add solemnity. You hold a book to facilitate prayer. You prepare the altar for the celebration of Eucharist. You do little things, but they help the other worshippers focus on their part. You help people say thanks to God, and in doing so you show your love.

Some servers take on larger responsibilities. Some Masses are so complex that they require the assistance of a master of ceremonies, a role also called by its abbreviation, MC. Many people hear "emcee" and think of talk show hosts or banquet speakers. But we use the same term in the liturgy. The head server who manages the details of Mass may be called the master of ceremonies. This role may be especially useful when a Bishop is present or for special celebrations such as those during Holy Week.

Pray while you serve. The more complex the ritual, the more the server will be tempted to disengage from the prayer and concentrate on the details of the ceremony instead. Good servers know these details so well that they can fulfill them while keeping their spirit centered on God. That is when you bring authenticity to your service—when you are thinking more about God than about serving.

History of the Server

At the Last Supper, someone had to set the table and prepare the meal. The servers are not mentioned, but unquestionably the very first Eucharist would have relied on servers. When the early Church gathered for the breaking of bread in homes, someone had to perform the same functions. In time the liturgy became more stylized, and so did its ministers.

Early Church

The distinguishing of various liturgical ministers was becoming necessary by the third century in Rome. An early collection of liturgical texts called the *Apostolic Tradition* differentiates between one group of ministers ordained through hand-laying and another group of people who were instituted or recognized for their gifts without hand-laying.[3] Some, but not all of these, carried out liturgical ministries.

The first person to mention the existence of acolytes in Rome is Pope Cornelius. One of his letters describes the number of ministers assisting him: 46 priests; 7 deacons; 7 subdeacons; 42 acolytes; 52 exorcists, lectors, and porters; and more than 1,500 widows and distressed persons.[4] Although Cornelius mentions the existence of acolytes, he does not say what they do. Given the evolution of this term according to its responsibilities, Cornelius probably meant those performing some kind of service at the altar and in the community—someone who assisted the deacon and the priest.

Middle Ages through the Second Vatican Council

The role of acolytes had become so important to the Church by the tenth century that the Roman–Germanic Pontifical included a ceremony for ordaining one. Elements of this ceremony probably existed several centuries earlier, but here it is included among the steps to priesthood ordination. Acolyte was the last of the four steps called minor orders, which preceded the major orders that concluded with priesthood. Only men were eligible to become acolytes, and only Bishops could ordain them to the role. During the ceremony the Bishop handed the new acolytes a candlestick and empty containers for the bread and wine, indicating the kind of altar service entrusted to them. The Bishop prayed that they might be filled inside with a spiritual light, like the candlelight that they would carry in their hands.[5] By the thirteenth century the acolyte was entrusted with administering Holy Communion to the faithful.[6]

Around the same time, it was becoming customary for a priest saying even the simplest Mass to have the assistance of an acolyte or some student who would proclaim the reading, make responses to the dialogues, and join in singing the chants.

The need for servers exceeded the number of available acolytes, so the Church developed a grassroots tradition of having students—and eventually young boys—serve Mass. These were not ordained to the order of acolyte, nor was it required that they be preparing for priesthood. Still, volunteering as a server inspired many boys to consider a vocation to the priesthood. A stereotype depicted an altar boy as a clean-cut, well-behaved, devout young man. This stereotype is still so powerful that "former altar boy" still appears in media-fueled resumes of heroes and villains to show the path of their destined glory or traumatic downfall.

Altar boys have traditionally dressed in cassock and surplice or alb and cincture. These vestments identified them as laypersons. The duties of servers included lighting and extinguishing altar candles, carrying cross and candles in processions, holding the thurible and boat for the incense, holding the missal for the priest, setting out cloths and vessels, holding the cruets of water and wine, and washing the hands of the priest.

Traditionally, altar boys also made responses at Mass. Today, when the priest says, "Lift up your hearts," everyone responds, "We lift them up to the Lord." In the centuries after the Council of Trent, however, servers conducted all these dialogues with the priest in a low voice in Latin, while the people prayed simultaneously in silence, usually from supplemental devotional materials. The longest of the responses is the one following the washing of the hands. The priest invites the people to pray, and they ask the Lord to accept the offering. Prior to the Second

Vatican Council, servers made the response, not the entire congregation. In Latin the priest's invitation was called the *Orate, fratres,* and the response was well known by its first word, *Suscipiat.* Once an altar boy had mastered the *Suscipiat,* he had climbed the highest hill of his responsibilities. It admitted him to an exclusive club of those who could rattle off this extended password.

Post–Second Vatican Council

After the Second Vatican Council the responsibilities of servers shifted. They were no longer required to learn the many responses in Latin because these were typically said in the vernacular. They did not have to recite the responses alone; all the people joined the servers. Other responsibilities were being shared by different ministers, so the role of server underwent a dramatic change.

Perhaps the most dramatic visible change was the admission of girls to the ranks of servers. The 1917 Code of Canon Law permitted women to serve Mass only at a distance when no men were present and for a just cause.[7] The revised Code of Canon Law implicitly gave girls permission to serve in 1983. Canon 230 §2 allowed all laypersons to perform a variety of liturgical functions. The Pontifical Council for the Interpretation of Legislative Texts explicitly interpreted the canon in 1992, saying that it did indeed permit girl servers, and Pope John Paul II personally concurred with the explanation.[8]

However, the precise ministry of acolyte was still reserved to men. In 1976 Pope Paul VI made some changes in the rituals known as steps to the priesthood. In the past, a man would be ordained to four minor orders, including acolyte, before being admitted to the major orders, including priesthood. Paul VI reached all the way back to the third-century *Apostolic Tradition* and restored the distinctions between instituted and ordained ministries. He abolished the four minor orders, but kept two of them—lector and acolyte—as instituted ministries. The ceremonies of institution still required the presence of a Bishop, and the candidate had to be male, but the man was no longer "ordained" to these ministries; he was instituted.

Paul VI no longer limited the ministry of acolyte to a candidate for the priesthood. The Bishop could install any layman into the ministry of acolyte. The acolyte accepted several responsibilities: to assist priests and deacons especially at the altar at Mass, to be extraordinary ministers of Holy Communion, to expose the Blessed Sacrament publicly for adoration and to replace it (though not to bless people with it), and to instruct the faithful who assume other liturgical duties.

However, this ceremony was not required for a layperson to assist at the altar; it was only required for those who wanted to be ordained a deacon or priest.[9] Women were excluded from the instituted ministry of acolyte, and only a Bishop could conduct the ceremony. These restrictions made it impractical for most parishes to rely on instituted acolytes for service at the altar. Consequently, the ministry of server has been widely and lawfully executed by willing men and women, boys and girls, who serve as lay ministers, although not formally instituted into the office by the Bishop.

The word *acolyte* has gone through its own evolution. Today it commonly means someone who carries a candle. It is used metaphorically—and not always complimentarily—for someone who is a dutiful, unquestioning supporter. The word is sometimes used for almost any minister assisting at the altar for Mass. Still, because the word *acolyte* has a specific meaning among instituted ministers, it is less precise to use it when referring to servers.

The extent of responsibilities of the instituted acolyte became clearer in 2006 when the Congregation for Divine Worship and the Disciple of the Sacraments interpreted the prevailing legislation to restrict the purification of vessels after Mass to priests, deacons, and acolytes.[10] Purification is not among the functions executed by more ordinary servers.

The *General Instruction of the Roman Missal* (GIRM) has surprisingly little to say about servers. The provisional English translation of 2002 uses the word *server* only three times—for their vesture,[11] the optional carrying of candles in the Gospel Procession,[12] and the optional ringing of a bell and swinging of the thurible during the Eucharistic Prayer.[13] All these uses of the word *server* translate to the Latin word *minister*, which appears dozens of additional times throughout the instruction. In all the other instances, it is translated with the cognate in English, *minister*. Hence, neither the original instruction nor its English translation is very clear about what servers do.

Consequently, the responsibilities of servers are spe
case, church by church, and priest by priest. Mass is the sa
where it is celebrated, but one of its most variable parts is th
for altar servers. The absence of more specific directions in the GIRM
and the presence of much local direction in parishes show the pastoral
care of the Church, which lets the specific duties of servers be determined where they are best known, evaluated, and appreciated: in the
local church.

Questions for Discussion and Reflection

1. How did you first become interested in becoming a server?

_____

_____

_____

_____

2. Who encouraged you to serve the Church in this way? Who
   are your role models for service?

_____

_____

_____

_____

3. What does Sunday Mass mean to you? Does your participation
   at Mass change when you are a server?

_____

_____

_____

_____

NOTES

1. *Kuriokon.*

2. *Catechism of the Catholic Church* (CCC), 1912.

3. See the *Apostolic Tradition*, 10–14.

4. See Cornelius, *Letter to Fabius*, from Eusebius *History of the Church* 6:43. Subdeacons assisted deacons. Porters locked and unlocked doors and had other custodial responsibilities.

5. See Roman–Germanic Pontifical 15:20–21.

6. See the Pontifical of Durandus 1:9, 3.

7. See canon 813 §2.

8. See *Acta Apostolicae Sedis* (AAS), 86 (1994):541; *Origins* 23 (April 28, 1994): 777–779.

9. See canon 1035.

10. See *General Instruction of the Roman Missal* (GIRM), 279; *Redemptionis sacramentum*, 119.

11. See GIRM, 339.

12. See GIRM, 175.

13. See GIRM, 150.

Spirituality and Formation of the Server

O God, you are my God—/ for you I long! / I look to you in the sanctuary / to see your power and glory.
—*Psalm 63:2, 3*

Reflection on your Role

Ministry comes from inside out. People will see you perform external actions, but these will have meaning only if they are accompanied by the internal action of prayer. While you serve Mass, keep a prayerful spirit about you. Let your ministry move from the inside out.

Remember what you are doing: you are participating at Mass. You hear and heed the word of God. You will share Holy Communion with your brothers and sisters in Christ. You carry Christ with you as you are dismissed from the liturgy. These attitudes will help you pray at Mass, and when you are praying at Mass, you will serve more meaningfully.

Think about some of the things you do as a server. Reflect on the sacred objects you hold and the actions you perform. Reconnect with their purpose and rededicate yourself to their mission.

Vesture

Some servers vest for Mass. Others do not. It depends on the local custom. You may wear a garment such as an alb, but it is not required.

Think about the different clothes you have at home. You use them for different purposes: for relaxation, for work, for exercise, and for making an occasion special. What do you usually wear to church? Where else do you wear those clothes? Do others dress the same way you do? On what occasions do you wear a uniform?

Ministers wear vestments at church as a sign of the sacred nature of the ritual, the season or day being celebrated, and to lend a degree of obscurity. The vestment of a server is usually something understated.

This avoids drawing attention to the person. When you wear an alb or other liturgical vesture, it covers you up to make you look plain, to tone down your body language, and to wrap you in a spirit of prayer. The vesture of servers intends to neutralize them, to make them blend into the visual harmony of the sanctuary, and to keep the worshipper's attention focused on more central parts of the liturgy—the word of God and the altar of our communion. How do you dress for serving? What difference do your garments make? When you change clothes, is there a change in you?

As you dress for Mass, try a prayer such as this:

> *God of all the earth,*
> *   you clothe the world in splendor*
> *   and make all creation shout praise to you.*
> *As I dress for Mass,*
> *   make me radiant with devotion,*
> *   that all who worship with me today*
> *   may give thanks to you.*

Vessels and Cloths

Before Mass you may be setting out the vessels for Holy Communion. During Mass you may be bringing them to the altar. These vessels will hold the body and blood of Christ.

You may arrange the bowls or ciboria that hold the bread for Mass, or the cups and chalices for the wine. You set out the cloths for the altar and the vessels, designating the space where they will rest and preparing for their cleansing. These containers and cloths resemble ones you use at home, but they are designated for a special purpose.

What kind of bread do you usually use at home? When you are ready for a meal, on what kind of plate do you place your bread? Do you drink wine at home? On what occasions? What kind of cup or glass do you use? When do you use cloth napkins? How about a tablecloth? Do some of your place settings have special significance? Are some designated for ordinary days and others for special days? Who sets the table at your home? What feeling do you have while you arrange a place for someone to eat?

As you prepare the vessels and cloths for Mass, try a prayer such as this:

> *Provident God,*
>> *you give us food and drink*
>> *to sustain our lives and bring us joy.*
> *As I prepare these vessels and cloths,*
>> *make me aware of your generosity,*
>> *so that all who hold and share your gifts*
>> *may become vessels of your very life.*

Processions

At various times during Mass you may join in a procession. The Entrance Procession brings all the ministers toward the altar. The Gospel Procession prepares for the solemn proclamation of the Good News of Jesus Christ. The procession with the gifts brings the bread and wine to the altar. The Communion Procession invites the faithful to share in the body and blood of Christ.

Cross

You may be carrying a cross in the Entrance Procession. This symbol of the crucified Jesus leads us into the church for our common prayer.

Where do you hang a cross at home? How do you use it? Does the image of the crucified Christ appear in some of your favorite prayer books? In your Bible? At church, how is Jesus represented on the cross? Is he fearful or triumphant? Pleading or confident? When you make the Stations of the Cross, do they invite you to a spirit of sacrifice? What do you think about when you make the Sign of the Cross?

When you carry the cross in procession, you are acting a little like Simon of Cyrene, who carried the cross for Christ,[1] and a little like Saint

Paul, who preached the crucified Christ to the world.[2] The master Jesus leads us into prayer, the crucified Jesus invites us to follow him, and the victorious Jesus helps us overcome the crosses in our lives.

When you pick up the cross to carry it, you might try saying a prayer such as this:

Almighty God,
  your Son Jesus Christ willingly came to us
  and took up a cross for our salvation.
As I lift up this cross,
  let me be mindful of its saving power,
  and help me sacrifice cheerfully
  for the sake of those your Son came to save.

Candles

You may be lighting candles for Mass, carrying them during the celebration, and extinguishing them afterward. Candles used to be the primary source of light in churches; now they are used for atmosphere and inspiration.

A candle melts beneath the fire. It completely spends itself in order to serve. As children of God we devote our lives to a similar purpose. We burn with the light of Christ so that others may experience the message of the Gospel. The fire of faith gives us purpose, and it shines within us even as the number of our days grows shorter. We spend our life for Christ until it is extinguished, and all that remains is memory on earth and light in heaven.

When do you use candles at home? For emergencies? To set a mood? Are there special occasions when you set them on your table? Do you still have your baptismal candle? When do you relight it?

When you carry a candle in the Entrance Procession, you accompany the cross of Christ as it leads the way ahead of the ministers and through the midst of the people of God. Your candles draw attention to the cross, not to you.

When you carry a candle in the Gospel Procession, you accompany the *Book of the Gospels* from the altar to the ambo. You stand near the ambo for the proclamation of the Gospel. When people look at the lector, you frame their view and focus their hearing. Your quiet service shows the importance of doing nothing else but listening to the words of Christ. When you hold a candle for the Gospel, listen to Christ, and his light will flood your inmost being.

When you light candles before Mass, you help prepare the Church to receive her King. When you extinguish them after Mass, you do it having just received Holy Communion, having just consumed Christ who is your light. You do not need candles. Christ burns within you.

When you pick up a candle, try a prayer such as this:

> *Lord Jesus Christ,*
> *Son of the living God,*
> *you came to be our light and our life.*
> *Dispel the darkness of my sin,*
> *make me radiant with faith,*
> *and draw all those who see this candle*
> *into the fire of your love and service.*

Incense

On special occasions at church we light incense to create a fragrance that induces prayer, and a smoke that rises to accompany petitions to the heavens. Incense may be used on any day, but we usually reserve it to draw attention to days of special significance.

To prepare incense you usually place charcoal bricks into the thurible and light them with a match. It often takes more than one try. Grains of incense rest in a separate container, the boat. At the appropriate times, you hand the priest the boat and lift the chain of the thurible. He spoons incense onto the burning charcoal, and the smoke and aroma fill the room.

What aromas fill your home? How does the house smell when food is being prepared? What else emits a fragrance there? Soap? Flowers? Candles? Do you use perfumes regularly? Or just on special days? How do you respond when someone smells nice?

You may use incense at church for the Entrance Procession, the Gospel Procession, the Preparation of the Altar and the Gifts, and during the Eucharistic Prayer. You may also use it to reverence the bodies of the dead at funerals.

The next time you prepare incense, you might say this prayer:

> *God, our maker,*
> *you delight in what you have made,*
> *and you fill the earth with pleasures*
> *for the eye, the ear, the mouth,*
> *the hand, and the nose.*
> *As I prepare this incense,*
> *let those who see its smoke*
> *and smell its perfume*
> *take delight in you*
> *and look forward to the day*
> *when your Son will draw them to himself.*

Movement

As the procession forms, you move. You go from point A to point B. You move from the door of the church to the sanctuary, from the altar to the ambo, from here to there.

Jesus moved around. Throughout his ministry he went to several towns and villages to meet the people, to proclaim his message, to heal the sick, and to recruit disciples. Then he went on to the next town.

Near the end of his life he made a solemn pilgrimage to Jerusalem. Saint Luke says he resolutely determined to go there.[3] On his way there, according to Luke, Jesus worked only a few miracles, but he said a lot to share his mind with those who would carry on his word and work.

Throughout the centuries the followers of Jesus have also made pilgrimages to holy places. Some have visited Jerusalem and Rome. Others revisit the place where their families began, the church where they were baptized, the place where they were married, or the cemeteries that hold their ancestors.

Whenever you join a procession at church, you fall in line with a train of Christians from every generation and place. Our desire to move from here to there is a symbol of our yearning to go from this life to the next. We make this journey behind the cross of Christ.

Where have you traveled lately? How do you prepare yourself for a journey? What prayers do you say on the way? What thanksgiving do you offer when you arrive?

When you join in the procession at your church, you might say this prayer:

> *Lord Jesus Christ,*
> *the Alpha and Omega,*
> *the beginning and the end,*
> *look kindly upon us whom you have called.*
> *Help us take up this procession in hope,*
> *walk it in faith,*
> *and reach our goal in love*
> *of you and of our neighbor.*

Singing

You sing when you process. The cantor, musicians, and choir will invite you and everyone to praise God in song. You won't be able to hold the music in your hand if you are carrying a cross, a candle, or incense, but you can still carry a song in your throat.

Music perfectly adorns the celebration of Mass. It sets a tone of praise and wonder, sorrow and contrition, hope and respect. It clothes our words and sentiments in ways that speech alone cannot.

✛ Great importance should therefore be attached to the use of singing in the celebration of the Mass, with due consideration for the culture of the people and abilities of each liturgical assembly. . . . [E]very care should be taken that singing by the ministers and the people is not absent in celebrations that occur on Sundays and on holy days of obligation.

—GIRM, 40

As a minister at the altar, it is especially important that you sing. You lift your mind and voice in prayer. You model for everyone else the importance of music. Whenever the assembly is asked to sing—whether it is in procession, in dialogue, in response, or in hymns—sing out in a strong, confident voice.

When do you have music at home? Do you just sing at birthdays or at other times of the year? What music do you listen to? When do you hear live music?

You might say the prayer below as you prepare to sing:

You have filled the earth with music, Lord;
the winds and seas, the birds and beasts
sound forth your majesty
throughout the world.
Hear my voice as I lift it to you.
Fill me with faith,
and fill this church
with the sound of your praise.

Holding the Book

At times the server holds the book for the priest or deacon standing at their chairs. The book, known as the Sacramentary or the Roman Missal, contains the main prayers of the Mass.

The missal is arranged in diverse sections. In the middle of the book you find the Order of Mass, the words and actions common to every celebration of Eucharist from the Sign of the Cross to the dismissal. The first part contains the prayers offered by the priest on set days throughout the liturgical year. The last part of the missal includes blessings, Masses for special needs and occasions, and a miscellany of other texts.

If you get to know the missal, it will help you appreciate the mysteries we celebrate at the altar. You will feel more a part of the liturgical year, and you will widen your prayer to a variety of needs that deserve your attention.

The main reason you hold this book during the service is so that the priest is free to extend his hands when he prays. Whenever the priest addresses God, he extends his arms in a position called *orans*, or praying. This posture was practiced from the early days of Christianity. Depictions of it appear in catacombs and tombstones from the first centuries of Church life. A person stands tall, head erect, arms up, and prays. The first Christians favored this posture because it already proclaimed a faith in the Resurrection, even before a word was said. They stood upright to pray, as they believed one day they would stand in Resurrection with Christ. To this day, Catholics stand for almost all the prayers of Mass. We sit for some of the readings and times of preparation. We kneel for parts of the Eucharistic Prayer. But we usually stand when we address God.

When you hold the book, you free the priest to assume the posture for prayer while he reads from the book. In some parishes, the book rests on a lectern or portable stand, and the server does not hold it. But if you do, you are helping the priest and everyone else pray. You should remember to pray too.

We rarely ever hold a book for someone else. Holding the book steady, and at the right height, may seem demeaning and a waste of human energy when an inanimate stand can do just as well—or better. But by putting your entire self at the service of this book and this prayer, you demonstrate to one and all the seriousness with which we take our prayer. We are willing to put our whole bodies, our minds, and our hearts at its service.

You could say this as you prepare to hold the book for Mass:

> *God of everlasting ages,*
>   *from one generation to the next,*
>   *your people have given you praise,*
>   *and many of their words*
>   *are honored in this book.*
> *As our community gathers for prayer,*
>   *we make these prayers our own.*
> *Fill us with your Holy Spirit.*
> *Make our prayer pleasing,*
>   *and help us put our entire selves*
>   *at the service of your Gospel.*

Liquids

As a server you will manage the cruets or other containers for the water and wine used at Mass. You will also wash the hands of the priest. Wine is usually carried in procession; water is usually kept at the side table. Together they define some of your responsibilities.

Water and Wine

During the Preparation of the Altar and the Gifts you help the priest set bread and wine on the table, and you offer him a cruet of water. He adds a bit of the water to the wine while he prays that we might share in the divinity of Christ who humbled himself to share in our humanity.

To perform this service you usually stand next to the altar with the water in your hand. The priest takes it from you and returns it to you. While he says his prayer quietly, you also join in a spirit of prayer.

You add water at home when you cook, clean, or garden. You may hold a hose, fill a pitcher, or pass a thirsty friend a bottle of water. You become a channel for the water. You help it accomplish its purpose.

When you hold a cruet at Mass, your ministry is quite visible. You strike a pose that people associate with the work of an altar server. It may seem that there is nothing special about it. But in your humility you save the priest a few steps so that he can concentrate on his prayer.

This prayer is for you:

> *Quietly I stand before you, O Lord,*
> *giver of life and origin of good,*
> *and I hold a vessel of water.*
> *Mixed with wine, this water becomes a sign*
> *of the Incarnation of your Son.*
> *May I be a sign of hope for this community,*
> *who long to live in his presence forever.*

Washing Hands

After the priest mixes water with wine, you wash his hands. You pour water over his hands into a bowl and offer him a towel. He dries his hands and returns the towel to you. In this ritual the priest prays that God will wash him of iniquity and cleanse him of his sins.

You wash your own hands at home, at work, and at school, of course, but you rarely wash someone else's hands. You may wash the hands of a child or an elderly person who is infirm. But adults usually wash their own hands.

Again, in this case, you have your own body do something that could be accomplished more simply. If the sanctuary came equipped with a sink, running water, and a towel, the priest could step over there and wash his own hands. But we do it differently at Mass. You become the wash stand. You put yourself at service.

It is humbling to do. But you are demonstrating this value to everyone: we put our whole lives to work for the Gospel, ready even to perform the simplest of tasks with the greatest of charity. We shouldn't have to tie someone else's shoe, wash her car, mow his lawn, or peel his orange. But when we do, we give him or her our time and our selves. Performing these actions for others does not require special skill, but it does require a willing heart. In a world where we rely on specialists to help us, and where we limit the kind of assistance we are willing to give, it is good on occasion to do something that anybody can do—like wash someone else's hands.

Here is a prayer for you:

Almighty God,
　　we are not worthy of you,
　　yet you have called us to your table.
Cleanse my heart inside and out;
　　make me a servant of all those in need.
May my actions help others pray
　　with clean hands and a pure heart.

Service at the Altar

Service at the altar requires a special spirituality. Pope Paul VI recognized this when he described the work of acolytes. Although he wrote with instituted acolytes in mind, his words apply beautifully to the work of all who serve at the altar: "Destined as he is in a special way for the service of the altar, the acolyte should learn all matters concerning public divine worship and strive to grasp their inner spiritual meaning: in that way he will be able each day to offer himself entirely to God, be an example to all by his seriousness and reverence in the sacred building, and have a sincere love for the Mystical Body of Christ, the people of God, especially the weak and the sick."[4]

Inner Spiritual Meaning

As you serve at Mass, come to a deeper understanding of the work you do, the signs and symbols you represent, and the objects you hold. They all have a deep spiritual meaning, and you can never completely explore them.

You carry this meaning with you while you serve. You hold within you your faith in God and your love for service. You help the priest when you know your work so well that you do not rely on him for cues. If he has to signal you, he is taking his mind off his own work. Help him by remembering and executing your work on your own as much as you can.

Live by the liturgical year. Celebrate feasts and seasons. Become familiar with the Sunday readings that form us in Christ. Learn the functions of the objects we use in the celebration of Mass.

Daily Offering of Self to God

Make daily prayer a habit. Make daily service a habit.

You may serve at Mass only on occasion, but make service and prayer a regular part of your life. At Mass you follow a routine. It doesn't change much from day to day. But in this routine you will meet the mystery of God. Because your work is familiar, you can worry about it less, and it can lead you to a deeper experience of God.

Many young people complain that Mass is boring because it is routine. But older people find Mass meaningful because it is routine. As with any repeated exercise, the more you do it, the more you appreciate it, the better you get at it, and the more it becomes a part of you.

Reverence in the Sacred Building

When you serve Mass your "office building" is the church. You work in God's house, and in a house made holy by the faith of many generations. Respect the church building.

As a server you will come to know the building, the closets where things are stored, and the function of public spaces. The building is flexible enough to house public prayer and private devotion, to celebrate the joy of a large wedding and the sorrow of reconciliation. Your respect and love for the building will demonstrate your respect and love for the other people who use it.

Sincere Love for the Mystical Body of Christ

Your service at Mass is a public example of the more private service you may be offering the mystical body of Christ, especially to the weak and the sick.

Pope Paul VI probably mentioned the weak and the sick because instituted acolytes bring them Holy Communion. Whether or not you are an extraordinary minister of Holy Communion, your service at the altar demonstrates your love for Eucharist, the body and blood of Christ, and for the body of Christ—the Church—who shares it.

The altar of sacrifice is also the table of our communion. You can support your service at church by taking seriously your service in the streets. When you help prepare a meal, stock a food pantry, share vegetables from your garden, visit the sick, or contribute to charities that provide social services, you are preparing yourself to serve Mass better. You are putting yourself at the service of Christ in sacrifice and meal.

Pope Paul VI also had this to say about instituted acolytes, and it applies to all who serve at the altar: "[The acolyte] will perform these functions more worthily if he participates in the holy eucharist with increasingly fervent piety, receives nourishment from it and deepens his knowledge of it."[5]

You can make no better preparation for serving than participating fully at Mass. Whether you are serving in the sanctuary or seated in the nave, give your mind and heart to Eucharist. Sing the songs meaningfully. Listen attentively to the word of God as it is proclaimed. Pray quietly with the priest during the Eucharistic Prayer. Share Holy Communion with your brothers and sisters.

When you celebrate Mass well, you will serve well. And when you serve well, you will celebrate well. The joys of heaven await you wherever you meet the body of Christ.

Questions for Discussion and Reflection

1. You "serve" Mass. In what other ways do you "serve" outside of Mass? Who receives your care? What do you do for them?

_____

_____

_____

_____

_____

2. On what occasions do you wear special clothing? How do those clothes make you feel? Do they change your attitude and your behavior? How?

_____

_____

_____

_____

_____

3. In your home, what are the most sacred objects? What makes them so? Do they represent certain people or events? Which ones?

_____

_____

_____

_____

_____

NOTES

1. See Matthew 27:32; Mark 15:21; and Luke 23:26.

2. See 1 Corinthians 1:23.

3. See Luke 9:51.

4. *Ministeria quaedam*, 6.

5. Ibid.

Serving the Liturgy

For these . . . servers, that the light of Christ may shine in their hearts, we pray to the Lord.

—Book of Blessings, 1853

The Server

✛ . . . lay ministers may be deputed to serve at the altar and assist the priest and the deacon; they may carry the cross, the candles, the thurible, the bread, the wine, and the water . . . .

—GIRM, 100

When the Church comes together to celebrate the liturgy, there is a need for dedicated ministers to take charge of certain responsibilities so that the celebrant can focus his attention on leading the assembly in prayer. These ministers are called servers. As a server, you need to know the layout and elements of the worship space, the vessels, the vestments, how to prepare the things needed for liturgy, and the order of service in order to assist with the ebb and flow of liturgical prayer. Here you will learn (or get reacquainted with) your role as a server—how to prepare vessels, how to move, how to carry things, how to be a model of liturgical participation, and how to keep stillness and silence.

A Walk through the Church

Basic Layout of Churches

As a server, you need to be very familiar with the layout of your church. The arrangement of the worship space varies greatly from church to church. For example, is the church where you serve in the basilica style, with one long, central aisle leading toward the sanctuary? Does your church have transepts, "arms" that branch off from the central nave to form the shape of a cross? Is the nave long and narrow and the ceiling high, perhaps with tall supporting columns? Or, does your building follow a more central plan, in which the nave takes a semicircular shape, with multiple aisles that lead toward the sanctuary? Or, is the seating area arranged in a monastic style: the assembly sitting along two sides of the church, facing each other, with the altar, ambo, and celebrant's chair elevated in the center?[1] The design, shape, and location of the ambo, altar, presidential chair, and font in your church building will affect how you function as a server in the liturgy. The following walk-through of the church focuses on the meaning and purpose of elements found in all churches. Be sure you know what's unique about your own church building.

> *Servers will need to be very familiar with the layout of the worship space. It is important to note that these arrangements will vary from church to church.*

The Church

What is the Church? First and foremost, the Church is a community, not a building. "Through his death and resurrection, Christ became the true and perfect temple of the New Covenant and gathered together a people to be his own. / This holy people, made one as the Father, Son, and Holy Spirit are one, is the Church, that is, the temple of God built of living stones, where the Father is worshiped in spirit and in truth."[2]

> ✚ The Church, in Christ, is a sacrament—a sign and instrument, that is, of communion with God and of the unity of the entire human race.
>
> —*Lumen Gentium, 1*

The Church, then, is not bricks and mortar, marble and stained glass, but people: people who, by their Baptism, have themselves become temples, dwelling-places of the Holy Spirit, and who have been gathered into one body to worship God. But the place where we gather for worship is important too—so important that we use the same word, *church*, to describe it.

Church buildings are like icons: they are rich in signs that point to something much bigger than themselves. Every aspect of the church building has something to teach us

> ✚ Because the church is a visible building, it stands as a special sign of the pilgrim Church on earth and reflects the Church dwelling in heaven.
>
> —*Rite of Dedication of a Church, 2*

about our faith. Towers, spires, steeples, and domes are visible from a long way off, and they constitute a visual invitation to join in worship. They remind us that we are a missionary people, called to spread the Good News both in word and in deed. Bells ring out a call to prayer, to recollection or rejoicing, to the whole community. Church doors invite all to enter. Vestibules or entryways provide a transition between the world without and the world within. Through art and architecture, the building itself tells the story of the journey of God's holy people "out of darkness into his wonderful light."[3]

The Nave

The main body of the church, where the assembly gathers, is sometimes called the nave. The word comes from the Latin word for *ship,* and refers to its shape. The early Church fathers loved this comparison of the Church to a ship. As we gather in the nave—this ark—we recognize that we are all in the same boat, so to speak: we are all on a voyage together. Jesus is with us, just as he was with the disciples, to calm the wind and the waves and to lead us to a safe harbor.

The nave is a place of activity and movement. When we gather for Mass, we are not an audience, but a liturgical assembly. Think of all the ways the assembly participates in Mass: singing and speaking the responses, standing and sitting together, listening to and meditating on the readings, kneeling to offer our prayers together with those of the priest during the Eucharistic Prayer, joining in the Communion procession. We are not passive observers, but active participants.

Through the nave run the aisles, which lead toward the altar. The aisles remind us that we are all on a holy journey together—a journey that will lead us one day to the altar of heaven. The nave, the place of the assembly, is an important part of the church building.

The Sanctuary

"The sanctuary is the space where the altar and the ambo stand, and 'where the priest, deacon, and other ministers exercise their offices.'"[4] The sanctuary is distinguished from the rest of the church, without being starkly separated from it. As a server, this is where much of your ministry happens.

THE ALTAR: The focal point of the sanctuary, and indeed of the entire church building, is the altar. At the altar a meal is shared, and Christ's saving sacrifice on the cross is renewed. "The Christian altar is by its very nature properly the table of sacrifice and of the paschal banquet."[5] The Church's prayer in dedicating an altar indicates how important the altar is, and how rich it is in meaning. The altar is "the Lord's table," "a sign of Christ," "a table of joy," "a place of communion and peace," "a source of unity and friendship," "the center of our praise and thanksgiving."[6]

Servers have the privilege of being close to the altar. You get to prepare the altar for the liturgy, and you often sit near the altar during Mass. By your reverent postures and actions—bowing when you approach the altar, and handling the vessels and linens to be placed on the altar slowly and carefully—you show that you understand what is happening in this holy place. And you become a living icon, helping to remind the entire assembly of the holiness of what we do when we celebrate Eucharist together.

THE AMBO: The ambo or pulpit is another privileged place in the church building. "Here the Christian community encounters the living Lord in the word of God and prepares itself for the 'breaking of the bread' and the mission to live the word that will be proclaimed."[7] In a way, the ambo is like the altar: both are tables where we receive the Lord. The altar is the table where we receive Christ in his body and blood. The ambo is the "table of God's word"[8] at which Christ comes to us through his word, proclaimed in the Gospel and the other scripture readings.

THE PRESIDENTIAL CHAIR: The presidential chair is an important place in the sanctuary. "The chair of the priest celebrant must signify his office of presiding over the gathering and of directing the prayer."[9] The chair is one of the central signs of leadership and teaching in the Church. The word *see* as in "Holy See" comes from the same Latin root as *seat* or chair (*cathedra*). Every Catholic diocese is centered around a cathedral church, which takes its name from the chair or *cathedra* of the Bishop.

Near the celebrant's chair are the chairs for other ministers—in particular, the deacon and any concelebrating priests, as well as servers. Servers have a special place, usually in the sanctuary, so that you can more easily carry out your ministry during the liturgy. But when you take those special seats set aside for you, remember that you also take on special responsibilities. Be sure to sit up straight. Keep your feet on the floor. Pay attention. Your special place, your seat, should remind you of the dignity of all the baptized, each of whom is called to a special place, a special responsibility in the world.

CREDENCE TABLE: The credence table is usually found in the sanctuary as well. This table holds the various vessels needed for the Mass—the chalice and paten, cups and plates for the distribution of Holy Communion, the cruet of water and the basin and pitcher for the handwashing, and linens. Following the Communion Rite, the credence table may also be used for the purification of the vessels.[10] Because the credence table is a holy place, it should not be used for other things—drinking water, musical instruments, stacks of hymnals—or servers' elbows!

TABERNACLE AND SANCTUARY LAMP: The tabernacle and sanctuary lamp may be located near the altar, or in a separate chapel. Catholics believe that Christ is truly present in the consecrated bread and wine received at Mass—and his presence does not cease when Mass is over, but rather abides as long as the elements of bread and wine endure. That is why the leftover hosts are reserved in a special place called a tabernacle. The tabernacle serves a practical function. Here ministers of care can come to pick up consecrated hosts so that those who are unable to join the community for Mass—the sick, the homebound, the imprisoned—can receive Holy Communion. But the tabernacle is also a focus for the prayer of the people before and after Mass. The tabernacle invites the faithful to encounter Christ, truly present in the Blessed Sacrament. Near the tabernacle, we find the sanctuary lamp, which burns day and night to "indicate and honor the presence of Christ."[11]

The Baptistry

THE FONT: The baptistry is another important place in the church building. This is where the baptismal font is located. "Through the waters of baptism the faithful enter the life of Christ. For this reason the font should be visible and accessible to all who enter the church building."[12] As we enter a church, we Catholics dip our fingers in holy water and make the Sign of the Cross: we remember our Baptism, echoing the words that were spoken over us at Baptism: "in the name of the Father, and of the Son, and of the Holy Spirit."[13]

THE PASCHAL CANDLE: The Paschal candle is a sign of the risen Christ. At the Easter Vigil, the candle is inscribed with the numbers of the current year. This is a powerful reminder that Jesus Christ, risen from the dead, is present here and now: "yesterday, today, and forever."[14] When the Easter season is over, the candle is placed near the font[15] and is lit whenever Baptism is celebrated, and for funerals as well. Both of these are celebrations of the Resurrection of Christ, in which we are sharers by our Baptism, and which gives us the hope of eternal life.

THE AMBRY: The ambry is the place where the oil of catechumens, the oil of the sick, and the sacred chrism are kept. It is often located near the baptistry, because two of these oils are used in the rites of Christian initiation.

Confessionals/Reconciliation Chapel

The confessionals (or Reconciliation chapel) are still another important place in the church building. Here the sacrament of Reconciliation takes place, and through the ministry of the Church we receive "pardon and peace"[16] and the forgiveness of our sins. Although the act of confession happens one-on-one with the priest, it is, like all the sacraments, about community. Sin separates us from God and from one another. Through the sacrament of Reconciliation, we are restored to communion and given new resolve to live in relationship with God and one another.

A Walk through the Sacristy

The sacristy is an important place for servers. In most parishes, it is the place where you prepare for your ministry: where you gather together with other servers, where you vest for the liturgy, where you receive your instructions and assignments, and where you also help to prepare the many things needed in the celebration of Mass.

Vestments

Vestments, both for clergy and for lay ministers, are generally kept in the sacristy. The most important of these vestments is the chasuble, which is worn only by the priest for the celebration of Mass. There are also stoles for the celebrant—a simple band of fabric that goes around

A dalmatic and stole.

A chasuble and stole.

A humeral veil and cope.

the neck and hangs down in front, worn under the chasuble. There are also vestments for the deacon: the dalmatic, which is a tunic in shape, and the diaconal stole, which is draped over the left shoulder and pinned at the right side. Chasubles, dalmatics, and stoles are worn in the liturgical colors: green for Ordinary Time; red for apostles and martyrs, and for certain solemnities like Pentecost; white and gold (and sometimes silver) for the Easter and Christmas seasons and for many saints' days; violet (and rose) for Advent and Lent.[17]

Among the other vestments in the sacristy, you will find copes. A cope is a mantle or cape, which clasps at the neck. It is worn for liturgies outside of Mass—for example, the Liturgy of the Hours—and for certain processions, like the procession of palms on Palm Sunday. Copes, too, are made in the liturgical colors, and they may be worn by a Bishop, priest, or deacon.

Albs, cassocks, and surplices are usually stored in the sacristy as well. The alb is the most ancient liturgical vestment—a long, white tunic reaching to the feet. It may be worn by all the ministers of the liturgy, both clergy and lay, and it is the usual vesture for altar servers. The surplice—the short white garment worn over a cassock, which may be black or some other color—is a later development of the alb, and is approved lay vesture in many places. The alb and the surplice are always white—a reminder of the white garment received on the day of Baptism. As you put on your alb or surplice to serve at Mass, you should remind yourself of the prayer that was spoken by the priest on the day of your Baptism: "See in this white garment the outward sign of your Christian dignity. With your family and friends to help you by word and example, bring that dignity unstained into the everlasting life of heaven."[18]

Your sacristy also contains humeral veils, used for Benediction of the Blessed Sacrament and for Eucharistic processions, as on Holy Thursday. This long, rectangular piece of fabric is fitted with clasps, so that (with the help of a server) the priest or deacon can attach it around his shoulders, and then place the ends of the veil around the monstrance or ciborium. (In cathedral churches, or in parishes, when the Bishop visits, humeral veils or vimpas are occasionally worn by the altar servers who hold the Bishop's miter and crosier.)

Linens

Linens of various kinds are also found in the sacristy. There are altar cloths, large white cloths that cover the altar during the celebration of Mass. There are corporals also, smaller white cloths that are placed over the altar cloth at the time of the Preparation of the Altar and the Gifts. The word *corporal* comes from the Latin word for *body*, because on this cloth the Body and Blood of Christ will rest. There are also purificators—small, white cloths that are used to wipe the edge of the chalice and communion cups during Holy Communion.

Here's one way to keep track of all these different linens: The altar cloth can be compared to a tablecloth, covering the entire altar table. The corporal is something like a placemat, for it is large enough to hold the chalice and paten. And the purificator is like the napkin. You will need all three when you set the altar for Mass.

In addition to the altar linens, there are hand towels, which are used for the ritual washing of hands of the priest during Mass, as well as for Baptism and anointings.

The pall is another special cloth used during the liturgy. This large, white cloth is placed over the casket at funerals; like the alb, it is a reminder of the white garment received on the day of Baptism. Also called a pall is a smaller, stiff, square piece of fabric sometimes placed over the chalice.

Because servers handle so many linens—whether the albs you wear or the altar cloth, corporal, and purificators—it is especially important that you wash your hands before you serve. This will help keep the linens clean and wrinkle-free. And the sacristan will be grateful!

Ritual Books

Also prominent in the sacristy are the ritual books used during Mass. Think of how Jesus began his active ministry in the Gospel according to Luke: by going into the synagogue, taking up the scroll, and reading the words of the prophet Isaiah.[19] Books are still central to our worship today. There are three principal books used during the Mass, all of which may be stored and prepared in the sacristy.

The Roman Missal (Sacramentary) contains the prayers for Mass: the Opening Prayer, the Penitential Act, the Prayer over the Gifts, the Eucharistic Prayer, the Prayer after Communion, and the Solemn Blessing, among others. It contains virtually every text prayed by the celebrant during Mass, except the readings, the Prayer of the Faithful, and the homily.

The Lectionary contains the readings for the Mass. There are different Lectionaries for Sundays and weekdays. On Sundays, the readings are arranged in a three-year cycle. In Year A, most of the Gospel readings are from Matthew's account. In Year B, we read from Mark and John. And in Year C, our readings are drawn from Luke. The arrangement of the Sunday Lectionary allows us to hear from the four evangelists almost in their entirety every three years, along with a good portion of the Old Testament and the New Testament letters.

The weekday Lectionary is arranged in a two-year cycle, which opens up the treasures of the Old and New Testaments even more fully. The Lectionary also includes dozens of readings for different kinds of celebrations—ritual Masses (Masses at which a special rite is celebrated—for example, Baptism, Confirmation, Holy Orders, or one of the Rites of Christian Initiation of Adults); wedding and funeral Masses; Masses for Various Needs and Occasions; and Masses in honor of the Blessed Virgin Mary and the saints.

The Book of the Gospels is a special book used on Sundays and other solemn occasions. It contains only the Gospel for Sundays, solemnities, feasts of the Lord, and other occasions. It is carried in procession, surrounded by candles, incensed, kissed by the priest or deacon, and given other signs of honor not given to any other book used during the liturgy. The Book of the Gospels is in fact treated much like the crucifix and the altar, because it, too, is a sign of Christ's presence in our midst.[20]

Vessels

There are many vessels kept in the sacristy that every altar server needs to be familiar with. The paten is the name for the plate used to hold the hosts during the celebration of Mass. Hosts may also be kept in ciboria, metal containers with lids, which come in many shapes and sizes.

Chalices, the cups used to contain the wine that will become the Precious Blood of Christ, also come in many different styles.

There are also cruets—small pitchers—which may hold the water and wine for Mass. A larger carafe may replace the wine cruet in the procession with the gifts, containing wine that is poured into the chalices at the altar before the Eucharistic Prayer begins. There are also basins and pitchers, used for the priest to wash his hands during the Mass, and sometimes at other times—for example, at Baptism or after anointings.

There are also bowls or basins used for the Rite of Blessing and Sprinkling Holy Water, which takes the place of the Penitential Act (Rite) at certain seasons of the year, especially during the Easter season. The sprinkler is also called an aspergillum. The aspergillum may be a natural branch, or it may be a specially made metal wand that is filled with blessed water.

A monstrance is a special receptacle in which a consecrated host is displayed for veneration. A monstrance is used for Exposition and Benediction of the Blessed Sacrament, and it may be carried in the procession with the Blessed Sacrament on occasions such as the solemnity of the Most Holy Body and Blood of Christ. Sometimes reliquaries containing the relic of a saint can be found in the sacristy.

Candles

The sacristy usually houses a variety of candles. From earliest times, light has played a significant part in Christian worship, which of course has its roots in Jewish worship. A seven-branched lamp stand of gold stood before the Ark and was kept burning at all times.[21] In the book of Revelation, "seven gold lampstands"[22] burn before the Lord.

The lighting of lamps in the darkness is a sign of hope in Christ, the true light. A symbol of Christ at the Easter Vigil is the Paschal candle. In the liturgy, candles are a sign of the presence of the risen Christ in our midst. Thus, candles are carried with the cross and the Book of the Gospels in the Entrance Procession, and lit candles around the altar. A candle burns before the Blessed Sacrament to mark Christ's presence in the Eucharistic bread reserved there, and at Exposition candles burn around the exposed sacrament.

Many of the rites of the Church include candles. A lit candle is presented to the newly baptized, a symbol of the light of Christ; and at funerals, the lighting of the Paschal candle is a reminder of the Resurrection. On February 2, the feast of the Presentation of the Lord, the entire assembly carries lit candles, and during the rites for the dedication of a church the lighting of candles on the altar and of special candles on the walls of the church is a "sign of rejoicing."[23] In many churches, candles are also lit before icons or images of saints. "Lights are at once a sign of joy, a reminder of a holy presence, and a symbol of the prayer to which they bear witness or to which they invite."[24]

Familiarize yourself with the candles that are used in your church. Candlesticks should be handled with great care. Clean hands will help highly polished candlesticks stay clean longer. Always hold lit candles upright; this will help keep dripping wax off the candle, off the floor, and off your alb.

Incense

Incense was an important part of Jewish worship. It was a symbol of prayer (think of Psalm 141) and was offered in the temple every morning and evening. It was used by Zechariah: while he is offering incense in the sanctuary of the Lord, the angel appears to announce the birth of John the Baptist.[25] Frankincense and myrrh are among the gifts the Magi offer to the infant Christ.[26] In the book of Revelation, the incense rising from the golden censer carried by an angel suggests "the prayers of all the holy ones."[27]

"Thurification or incensation is an expression of reverence and of prayer."[28] Incense is carried in procession, and it is used to incense the altar, the cross, the Book of the Gospels, the gifts on the altar, the celebrant, the assembly, and the consecrated bread and wine. In the liturgy, incense directs our attention to the holy, to the presence of God.

The server who handles the thurible and boat (the small container holding the incense itself, so called because of its shape) needs to take special care in handling the coals. Know how many are needed at the beginning of Mass, and know when the coals need to be cleaned and replenished. Use caution whenever you light coals, and always do so in the designated safe place—not over carpet or near flammable items. Handle the thurible itself with care, and know how to open it smoothly and gracefully when the celebrant adds incense to it.

The Sacrarium

The sacrarium is a distinctive feature of a well-equipped sacristy.

> The sacristy near the sanctuary will usually contain the *sacrarium*, the special sink used for the reverent disposal of sacred substances. This sink has a cover, a basin, and a special pipe and drain that empty directly into the earth, rather than into the sewer system. After Mass, when the vessels are rinsed and cleansed, the water is poured into the sacrarium so that any remaining particles that might be left will not be poured into the sewer but will go directly into the earth. When the purificators and corporals are rinsed before being washed, the water is disposed of in the sacrarium. The sacrarium also can be used to discard old baptismal water, leftover ashes, and the previous year's oils, if they are not burned.
>
> In addition, if any of the Precious Blood is accidentally spilled during Mass, it is carefully wiped up and the area is washed. The water from this process also should be poured down the sacrarium. Reverence for sacred things continues even after they are no longer useful in the liturgy.[29]

The Role of the Server

Servers have a number of significant liturgical responsibilities. You may serve on your own during daily Mass; more frequently, you'll be part of a team during Sunday Mass or other special rites such as Confirmation, weddings, or funerals. Depending upon the nature of the celebration, the team could number as few as two or three, or as many as seven—or even more! "If there are several persons present who are able to exercise the same ministry, nothing forbids their distributing among themselves and performing different parts of the same ministry or duty."[30] When assigning responsibilities, liturgical coordinators need to keep in mind that servers cannot perform two distinctive functions at the same time. When a team serves together on a regular basis, it can be easy to get into a rut. Vary the tasks as much as possible from week to week, so that everyone can learn to do the various tasks.

The following roles are divided among the servers:

- Altar Assistants

- Book-bearers

- Candle-bearers

- Cross-bearer

- Thurifer

Typically during Sunday Mass, two servers function as **altar assistants**. Their primary function is to prepare the altar for the celebration of Eucharist. Servers prepare the altar with the corporal, the Roman Missal, the chalice, communion cups, and purificators (and pall if used). The altar assistants may go with the celebrant to greet the gift bearers and help place the bread and wine (and possibly water) upon the altar; and they may take the people's offerings of money (the collection) to be placed near the altar. The altar assistants also present the cruet so that the priest or deacon can add water to the wine at the preparation of the gifts; they bring the bowl, pitcher, and towel to the celebrant for the washing of hands. The altar assistants also help with clearing the altar following the Communion Rite.

As **book-bearers**, servers hold the Roman Missal (Sacramentary), other ritual books (the *Book of Blessings*, for example, or the *Rite of Christian Initiation of Adults*), or ritual binders for the celebrant during Mass or other rites. This helps the celebrant pray ritual texts more easily and enables him to assume the orans position, an ancient posture for prayer, with both hands extended. Servers usually hold the Roman Missal (Sacramentary) during the Opening Prayer and Prayer after Communion. However, there may be other times when this is necessary; for example, during the Penitential Act (Rite), the Creed, or the Solemn Blessing. Your liturgical ministry coordinator will instruct you.

Candles may be carried during the Entrance Procession, with the cross and the Book of the Gospels, and with the cross during the procession at the end of Mass. **Candle-bearers** may also accompany the Gospel procession. Candle-bearers should hold their candles with both hands, with dignity and reverence. Candle-bearers should hold their candles at the same height.

A cross with a corpus is carried during the processions at the beginning and end of Mass. The **cross-bearer** leads the procession and sets the pace for it (except when the procession is led by the thurifer). The cross-bearer needs to be confident about the processional route and should walk slowly and with dignity.

The server responsible for incense is called a **thurifer**. Incense is carried in a vessel called a thurible. The words *thurifer* and *thurible* come from the Greek word *thuos*, meaning "sacrifice." A thurifer may be assisted by another server who carries the incense boat.

The Server at Mass

The celebration of the liturgy—in particular, the celebration of Eucharist—is the most important thing we do when we gather as a Christian community. It is the "summit" of all we do as Church, the greatest of all our prayers.[31] At the same

> ✠ The liturgy is the summit toward which the activity of the Church is directed; at the same time it is the fount from which all the Church's power flows.
> —*CSL, 10*

time, Eucharist is the "fount," the source from which we draw strength for everything else we do: whether teaching the faith or serving the poor or speaking out for justice and peace.[32] When we gather for Sunday Mass, we should do so with an awareness that what we do is important— the most important thing we do all week. At the same time, when we come to Mass, we should come with open hearts and minds, ready to hear what God will say, and to bring God's word to life in our daily lives. The celebration of Eucharist and the sacramental reception in Holy Communion are meant to transform us. For Christians, conversion is not a one-time event; it is a process that lasts a lifetime.

Mass is one great prayer, the prayer of the Church offered to God the Father in the name of Jesus Christ, by the power of the Holy Spirit. But this one prayer is divided into many parts, and in the course of Mass we offer many different kinds of prayers to God: prayers of sorrow for sin, prayers of praise and thanksgiving, and petitions for ourselves and for the whole world. Mass can be divided into four main parts: the Introductory Rite, the Liturgy of the Word, the Liturgy of the Eucharist, and the Concluding Rite. The following pages will walk you through preparations for Mass, the Mass itself, and clean up after Mass.

Preparing for Mass

A dedicated server should arrive early enough to prepare spiritually, assist with the setup of the worship space, and to vest. Twenty to thirty minutes early is usually sufficient, but at certain celebrations you may need to arrive earlier.

When arriving at church, be sure to check in with the coordinator of your ministry. This will vary from parish to parish, but it could be the celebrant, liturgical coordinator, pastoral associate, or the sacristan. Some parishes have a check-in sheet in the sacristy for you to check off your name when you arrive. Always remember: if you can't make your scheduled liturgy, try to find a replacement or call ahead.

Verify your responsibilities (cross-bearer, candle-bearer, book-bearer, altar assistant, thurifer) with the coordinator of your ministry. You will probably be assigned to perform one or more of these duties.

> **Things to Remember:**
>
> • *Your ministry as a server begins even before Mass does.*
>
> • *Arrive early.*
>
> • *Check in with whomever coordinates your ministry.*
>
> • *Find your alb.*
>
> • *Know your responsibilities.*
>
> • *Be aware of any special rites.*
>
> • *Be sure you know what you are doing, and when and how to do it before Mass begins.*
>
> • *Know where everything is kept that you will need as you serve (candles and cross, thurible, if it is to be used, vessels, vestments, linens, and matches).*
>
> • *Be prepared!*
>
> • *And, of course, pause for prayer.*

Check to see if anything unusual is happening today: one of the rites in the RCIA, infant Baptism, a special blessing, and the like. Know if other books, beyond the Roman Missal (Sacramentary), will be used. Find out if you will need to hold these books during the liturgy for the celebrant.

Get vested. Depending upon your diocese or parish community, servers wear either an alb or a cassock and surplice.[33] Sometimes the alb is bound at the waist with a cincture, which is something like a belt. Make sure your alb or cassock is neither too short nor too long. Ankle-length is usually just about right.

Servers can often help with other preparations as well. While the sacristan will take care of most of the Mass preparations, it is always good for servers to check in and see if help is needed, especially with putting vessels and linens on the credence table and offertory table, and lighting candles.[34] (Be sure to wash your hands before handling the vessels and linens of Mass.) When setting up for Mass (or other rites and services), remember to be reverent and quiet, walking slowly and deliberately, so as not to disrupt the prayer and meditation of the assembly. The candles at the altar should be lit 10 to 15 minutes before Mass begins. Do so slowly, reverently, and quietly, genuflecting before the tabernacle, bowing before the altar. Don't use a match—or, worse yet, a cigarette lighter in the presence of the assembly. It's best to use the brass candlelighter. If incense is used, it should also be lit about 10 to 15 minutes before the Entrance Procession.

Before Mass begins, the **credence table** should be prepared with the following:

- the corporal to be placed on the altar at the Preparation of the Altar and of the Gifts;

- chalice, communion cups, and purificators;

- additional ciboria;

- the cruet containing water to be mingled with the wine;

- the pitcher, basin, and towel for the washing of hands during the Preparation of the Altar and of the Gifts;

- a vessel of water and aspergillum, if there is to be a Rite of Blessing and Sprinkling Holy Water.

The following items should be arranged and placed on the **offertory table**, which is usually located in the nave of the church:

- paten with the proper amount of hosts to be consecrated, including hosts for the faithful and the larger host for the celebrant;

- cruet or carafe with the proper amount of wine to be poured in the chalice and communion cups for consecration.

The sacristan or priest usually prepares the Book of the Gospels, Lectionary, and Roman Missal (Sacramentary) before Mass begins. The deacon (or when there is no deacon, a lector) carries the Book of the Gospels in the Entrance Procession. The Lectionary is placed at the ambo before Mass.[35] The Roman Missal and any ritual texts to be used by the celebrant are usually placed near the presidential chair or on the credence table, close to the server who will present them to the celebrant.

As a server, you need to model full, conscious, and active liturgical participation.[36] Be sure you have access to a worship aid or hymnal to use during Mass. If you are unable to carry the resource needed for the Entrance Song because you will be holding or carrying other items (cross, candles, incense), place the hymnal or worship aid near your chair, and glance at the song before Mass begins. Often, you'll find that you can sing along even without the resource.

Between preparing for your ministry and getting vested, be sure to take a few moments to collect your thoughts and pray before Mass. You might find the prayers on pages 16–26 helpful for your own preparation. In some parishes, the celebrant and liturgical ministers gather in the sacristy or in the vestibule immediately before Mass for a short prayer. The priest asks for God's blessing on all ministers and the community, and that the celebration of Eucharist benefits the lives and faith of all who participate.

You should be in place for the Entrance Procession about ten minutes before the Mass begins. This allows plenty of time for final preparations (preparing the cross, lighting coals for incense, readying the processional candles, etc.). Be sure that you are lined up in proper processional order. During this time, you can also assist the ushers and greeters while people come into the church. Greet them with a welcoming smile and a "hello."

How do you know when the procession starts? Many parishes have a familiar "signal" that is used to let the musicians know that the procession is ready to begin. Typically this is an exchange between the priest, liturgist or sacristan, and the director of music or primary accompanist. This signal might be a subtle nod of the head or a wave of the hand. In large church buildings, where the main doors are quite far from the music ministers, it works well to have the ministers remain out of sight, in the vestibule, until the entire procession is lined up and ready. That way, the entrance of the cross into the body of the church is a visible sign that the entire procession is ready. Be familiar with the "signal" in your own parish.

Serving during Mass

INTRODUCTORY RITE: The liturgy begins with the Entrance Procession. This procession completes the gathering of God's people, which has already begun as the faithful have arrived at the church and have taken their seats for the celebration of Mass. The procession—led by the cross-bearer (or, sometimes the thurifer)—suggests the procession of God's people through history, led by Jesus on a journey leading to the heavenly city. The procession is orderly, with servers, lectors, deacons, and priests taking their particular place according to their particular role. The procession should remind us of the variety of gifts that the community brings to the celebration of the liturgy: "there are different forms of service but the same Lord."[37]

In the Entrance Procession, servers carry the cross and the incense; they also carry candles around the cross and the Book of the Gospels, which is carried by the deacon, or, when there is no deacon, a lector.

The following is a very simple order of procession:

Candle-Bearer   Cross-Bearer   Candle-Bearer

Other Servers / Ministers

Deacon or Lector with
Book of the Gospels

Celebrant

On solemnities, the procession may be more elaborate, involving more servers:

Thurifer

Candle-Bearer   Cross-Bearer   Candle-Bearer

Other Servers / Ministers

Master of Ceremonies

Candle-Bearer   Deacon or Lector with   Candle-Bearer
Book of the Gospels

Celebrant

When the Bishop is present, then the procession will usually be more embellished. The following is a typical order of procession when a Bishop is present:

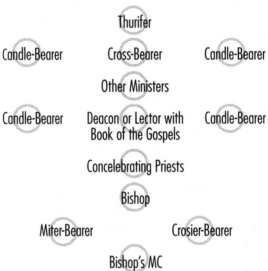

Thurifer

Candle-Bearer   Cross-Bearer   Candle-Bearer

Other Ministers

Candle-Bearer   Deacon or Lector with   Candle-Bearer
                 Book of the Gospels

Concelebrating Priests

Bishop

Miter-Bearer   Crosier-Bearer

Bishop's MC

When you process, be mindful of the liturgical space. If you process too close to the other ministers, the procession can look sloppy and disorganized. If you are too far apart, it might not look like a procession at all! Most parishes have a rule of thumb for spacing the procession. For example, "when the minister in front of you reaches the third pew, begin to walk" or "count four paces and then begin to walk." For great solemnities when many ministers join the procession, a master of ceremonies might stand near the doors to "space" the procession as it enters the church.[38] Consult with your liturgical ministry coordinator to learn of the preferred practice in your parish. Regardless of the method, all ministers should be in sync with one another. Some things to keep in mind: maintain a constant pace during the procession. If you speed up or slow down, you can throw off the pace of the procession. Maintain the distance between you and the ministers in front of you—it's not a race, and you don't need to catch up!

If incense is used, the thurifer leads the procession. Ask the celebrant to add incense to the thurible just before the procession begins. Gently swing the thurible as you walk. Most thuribles have a metal ring at the top of the chain holding the vessel. Slip your thumb through the ring and then grasp the chain with closed fingers—almost like clenching a fist. Bend your elbow, raising the thurible high enough—so that it is away from the floor (you don't want to bang the thurible on the floor as you're leading the procession). The thurible should swing out in front of you and then behind you. Use a gentle motion, swinging your arm at the shoulder while keeping your elbow bent.

During the procession the thurifer will lead the procession, swinging the thurible gently as he or she processes. Once the thurifer reaches the sanctuary, he or she will stand aside as the other ministers come forward, reverence the altar, and go to their places.

Once the priest (and the deacon if there is one) reaches the sanctuary, he will go around the altar and reverence it with a kiss. Then the priest will incense the altar and cross. If there is a deacon, he will assist the server as the priest puts incense in the thurible, takes the thurible, and walks around the altar while incensing. When the priest (and the deacon if there is one) has finished, the thurible will be returned to the thurifer, who then takes it to the sacristy or other designated place, until it is needed for the Gospel Procession.[39]

When you serve as the cross-bearer in the procession, be sure you know the custom in your parish for the placement of the cross during the celebration of Mass. The celebration of Mass requires the presence of a crucifix. Sometimes the processional cross is that crucifix, and it remains in the sanctuary throughout Mass. In parishes that have a crucifix permanently fixed in the sanctuary, the processional cross usually does not remain in the sanctuary but is placed in another location following the Entrance Procession. Be aware of the custom in your parish.

The candle-bearers and cross-bearer usually bow their heads in unison upon reaching the foot of the sanctuary, then continue to the place where the candles and cross are normally placed during the

The celebration of Mass requires a crucifix.

Mass. In some places the cross-bearer goes first, bows his or her head, and then the candle-bearers do the same. This may depend upon the width of the aisle.

After you have carefully placed the thurible, cross, and candles in the designated places, go to your seats in the sanctuary. The Sign of the

Cross and the Penitential Act (Rite) follow. With these rites, the entire assembly is reminded of who we are: People of God, marked with the Sign of the Cross, baptized in the name of Christ. We acknowledge our failings, and we give God praise for his mercy.

During the Easter season, and on other occasions, the Penitential Act can be replaced with the Rite of Blessing and Sprinkling Holy Water, in which water is blessed and sprinkled over the entire assembly as a reminder of Baptism. Servers often assist the priest with this rite. One server usually holds the Roman Missal (Sacramentary), from which the priest reads the prayer of blessing of holy water. (Be sure you know which ribbon to open the book to). Another server holds the vessel filled with water to be blessed, which should be prepared before Mass begins and placed on the credence table. Know when to come forward and stand before the priest for the blessing of the water. Sometimes the priest will do this himself. Be sure to check with your liturgical ministry coordinator.

When you carry the vessel of holy water, walk close to the priest, usually on his right, as he makes his way through the assembly to sprinkle the people. Your main task is to make it easy for the priest to dip the aspergillum (the sprinkler) or branch into the vessel as he sprinkles the people.

After the priest has finished sprinkling the assembly, the server takes the vessel and the aspergillum and returns it to the credence table or sacristy, as directed.

On Sundays, solemnities, and feasts, the Gloria is sung or said immediately following the Penitential Act.[40] This is an ancient and wonderful prayer of praise of the God who gave us Jesus as our Savior. The Opening Prayer comes after the Gloria.[41] It is also called the "collect," because it "collects" or gathers all the prayers of the assembly into one. This prayer is found in the Roman Missal. If you are responsible for opening the book to the right page, be sure you know which ribbon marks the Opening Prayer.

What is the best way to hold the book for the celebrant? Here is one of many options:

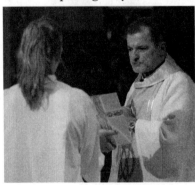

Hold the book or ritual binder firmly and steadily.

• Hold it in front of you, with one hand under each side of the book.

- Hold the book out from your body, slightly raised or angled up from the bottom to allow a clear sight line for the celebrant.

- Hold the book firmly and steadily, but do not be so stiff that the priest cannot adjust the book if you do not get the book at the right angle for him.

- If the celebrant's chair is placed on a platform, you may need to hold the book higher.

- Be sure to check with the celebrant to see if he has a preferred way for you to hold the books.

- Wait until the celebrant has finished the prayer completely and all (including you) respond "Amen" before returning the Roman Missal to the credence table or other designated place.

If there are a large number of children in the assembly, there may be a separate children's Liturgy of the Word. Is there a special ritual text for the calling and sending of the children? Does a cross lead them to the place where they'll share the word together? Know what the custom is in your parish.

LITURGY OF THE WORD: After the Opening Prayer, all are seated. The reader goes to the ambo, and the Liturgy of the Word begins. With the entire assembly, the servers listen attentively to the scripture readings, in which God speaks to his people, and they join in singing or saying the Responsorial Psalm. At some point during the Liturgy of the Word, servers will need to prepare the candles and incense (if it is to be used) for the Gospel procession. Know when you are supposed to get ready, and move in unison with the other servers.

Following the Second Reading, the Acclamation before the Gospel is sung, and the entire assembly stands. The word *Alleluia* comes from Hebrew and means "praise God." Even in Lent, when the Alleluia is not sung, we sing an acclamation of praise. The Gospel is about to be proclaimed to us—this is Good News! The candle-bearers, and on solemn occasions, the thurifer, lead the deacon or priest to the altar where the Book of the Gospels was placed at the beginning of Mass, and then accompany him to the ambo. During the proclamation of the Gospel, the candles and the incense bring special honor and attention to these sacred words.

Depending on the custom in your parish, and the season of the year, the procession with the Book of the Gospels may be as simple as the deacon or priest processing with the book alone to the ambo. Or it may be more elaborate, with candle-bearers and thurifer accompanying the procession. The processional route may also be simple or elaborate, depending on your community and on the liturgical season as well. Be aware of the custom in your parish and of any special solemnities or feasts that may affect how the Gospel procession takes place.

No matter how the Gospel procession happens in your parish, here are some things to be aware of.

When incense is used, the thurifer will need to prepare the thurible before the Gospel (during the Responsorial Psalm is a good time to do this). The coals that were used for the Entrance Procession may be almost burned out by this time. Clean the coals, and add another charcoal and light it so that it is glowing before the proclamation of the Gospel begins. Please note: the whole charcoal doesn't have to be glowing red. As long as the majority of it has been lit, this will be enough for the incense to burn. These preparations should happen in a fire-safe place, not in the sanctuary in view of the assembly.

As the priest or deacon places the Book of the Gospels on the ambo, the candle-bearers take their place on either side of the ambo.

As the Acclamation before the Gospel begins, the thurifer brings the thurible and the boat containing the incense to the celebrant. The server will open the thurible, and the priest places incense on the coals. The priest goes to the altar, takes the Book of the Gospels, and holds it high. (If there is a deacon, he will first go to the priest for a blessing, then go the altar to get the Book of the Gospels). At the same time, the candle-bearers move to stand before the altar, where the Book of the Gospels has been placed.

The thurifer and candle-bearers lead the priest or deacon along the designated processional route to the ambo. During the procession, the servers should join in singing the acclamation. Remember, the servers are part of the liturgical assembly, and as such they are not only *serving* the liturgy, but they are also *praying* the liturgy. Their example of active participation is an example for the whole assembly.

As the priest or deacon places the Book of the Gospels on the ambo, the candle-bearers take their place on either side of the ambo. The thurifer stands close by, ready to hand the thurible to the priest or deacon. The priest or deacon gives the liturgical greeting to the assembly: "The Lord be with you." The people, including the servers, will respond. The priest or deacon then announces the Gospel ("A reading from the holy Gospel according to [N.]" to which all respond, "Glory to you, Lord.").[42] The thurifer hands the thurible to the priest or deacon who incenses the Book of the Gospels. After the incensation, the priest or deacon hands the thurible back to the thurifer. All servers remain in place at the ambo until the conclusion of the Gospel reading.

After the Gospel, the assembly is seated. The servers return the candles and incense to the appropriate place and take their seats. All listen attentively to the homily, in which the priest or deacon breaks open the word that was just proclaimed, and helps to connect it with our daily lives.

After the homily, if there are catechumens (people preparing for Baptism) in your parish, they are dismissed. Sometimes they are led from the assembly by a server with a cross. Know what the custom is in your parish community.

The Liturgy of the Word continues with the Creed, which all recite together, professing common faith. Then, in the Prayer of the Faithful, all petition God for the needs of the Church, the world, those in need, and the local community. You may need to hold a ritual text for the celebrant during the Prayer of the Faithful. Know what the custom is in your community.

LITURGY OF THE EUCHARIST: The Liturgy of the Word concludes with the Prayer of the Faithful. Then comes the Liturgy of the Eucharist, which begins with the Preparation of the Altar and of the Gifts. The servers help to prepare the Lord's altar for the holy meal.

The servers place the altar, chalice, communion cups, purificators, and Roman Missal on the altar. If there is a deacon present, he stands at the altar and the servers hand him each of these items, which he arranges on the altar. If there is no deacon, the servers spread out the corporal and place the chalice and the book upon it. Know which page to open the book to, and be sure it is marked with a ribbon.

After preparing the altar, servers usually assist the celebrant or deacon in receiving the gifts brought forward by the assembly—the bread and wine, and also the monetary gifts of the assembly. The gifts are handed directly to the priest or deacon, who may then hand them to the servers to be placed at the altar. On solemn occasions, the members of the assembly who are to present the gifts may be led forward by servers carrying a cross and candles.

As the gifts are being received, or immediately following, the servers prepare for the rites that surround the Preparation of the Altar and of the Gifts. A cruet of water is presented to the celebrant (or the deacon, if he is present), who mingles a small amount of water with the wine that has been brought forward by the assembly. This small rite has profound meaning, as the quiet prayer that accompanies it reveals: "by the mystery of this water and wine may we come to share the divinity of Christ, who humbled himself to share in our humanity."[43]

If incense is used, it is presented to the celebrant after the elevation of the chalice. The celebrant blesses the incense and adds a small amount to the thurible. Then he incenses the gifts upon the altar and then walks around the altar, incensing it as well. Then he incenses the cross. The deacon, or, if no deacon is present, the thurifer, takes the incense and incenses the celebrant, followed by the assembly, for we, too, are a sign of Christ's presence.

If there is no deacon, the thurifer takes the incense and incenses the celebrant, followed by the assembly.

Servers then bring forward a basin, pitcher, and towel for the celebrant to wash his hands. This is another significant rite, as is evident from the accompanying quiet prayer of the priest, which echoes Psalm 51: "Lord, wash away my iniquity, and cleanse me from my sin."[44] Two servers could assist with this ritual act (one carrying the cruet or pitcher of water and bowl and the other carrying the towel), or one server could assist (carrying the cruet/pitcher of water in one hand, the bowl in the other with the towel draped over one arm).

Now the altar and the gifts are ready, and the priest prays the Prayer over the Gifts, bringing together the hopes and desires of the assembly as the Eucharistic Prayer, the heart of Mass, begins.

The Eucharistic Prayer begins with the preface dialogue, ancient words that have been part of the Christian liturgy for centuries: "Lift up your hearts."[45] The preface, which follows, is a prayer that praises God for the salvation Jesus Christ won for us. The preface gives us good reason to join in the "Holy, Holy, Holy,"[46] the song of the angels and saints. Join the assembly in singing this great song with heart, mind, and voice.

Depending on the custom in your parish, servers may kneel and ring bells at the elevation of the host and the chalice. Sometimes the thurifer incenses at the elevations as well. Whatever the custom is in your community, the Eucharistic Prayer is a time to join the entire assembly in praying with the priest.[47]

After the Eucharistic Prayer, the assembly stands, and the Communion Rite begins with the Lord's Prayer. The sign of peace flows out of the prayer for forgiveness in the prayer of Jesus: "forgive us our trespasses, as we forgive those who trespass against us."[48] After the exchange of peace is the fraction rite, as the celebrant breaks the consecrated host. This rite is accompanied by a litany that is sung or spoken: "Lamb of God, you take away the sins of the world: have mercy on us. . . ."[49] The priest holds up the consecrated bread and wine for all to see, and then he, and those present, receive Holy Communion.

Servers generally receive Holy Communion shortly after the priest and deacon. Know what the custom is in your community, and be focused and reverent as you approach the altar to receive the Body and Blood of Christ. People in the assembly will be watching what you do as a model of how to receive communion reverently.

Servers often assist with clearing the altar during the Communion Rite, or immediately following it, removing the Roman Missal and preparing it for the Prayer after Communion, and sometimes removing the vessels as well. Know what the custom is in your parish community.

Following Holy Communion, the assembly may meditate in silence for a few moments. Use this time to meditate along with them, not to get ready for the next thing you need to do. Silence and stillness have their own part in the liturgy.

Some parishes sing a hymn of praise following Holy Communion. If this is the custom in your parish, be sure to sing alone. The Prayer after Communion follows, and then it is time to prepare for the Concluding Rites, which include the greeting ("The Lord be with you"[50]), the blessing, and the dismissal.

CONCLUDING RITE: The procession at the beginning of Mass has many layers of meaning. It symbolizes the gathering of God's people for worship, and it suggests the variety of ministries in the Church. It is also an emblem of the pilgrim journey we are making together in the footsteps of the Lord. The procession at the end of Mass is also richly symbolic. The last words we hear at Mass are words of sending: "The Mass is ended; go in peace to love and serve the Lord."[51] We aren't simply let out, as when the bell rings at the end of the school day. We are sent—we are given a mission and a task, to take the Gospel we have heard and the sacrament we have shared into the world, and to let it grow and live in us in our daily lives, not just in church on Sunday. In the procession at the end of Mass, therefore, we do not just go back where we started. We begin a journey to a new place—wherever God may send us. The reverence, joy, and energy you bring to your ministry as servers can help the entire assembly to feel what this procession is all about.

Know when to prepare for the procession out of the sanctuary. If a hymn is sung at the time of the procession, you may stand and sing a verse or two before processing out. Or, if a choir or an instrumentalist accompanies the procession, you may need to be ready to move immediately following the dismissal. The ministers process out of the church in the same order they processed in. The Book of the Gospels, however, is not carried in the procession at the end of Mass. Incense is also not called for during the procession at the end of Mass.

Candle-Bearer   Cross-Bearer   Candle-Bearer

Other Servers / Ministers

Celebrant

Where you line up for this procession will vary from parish to parish. Be sure you are aware of your parish custom. In most cases you will line up at the side of the sanctuary, wait for the priest and/or deacon to move from the presidential chair to reverence the altar, and then lead them out of the sanctuary. Know the processional route. Just as you do for the Entrance Procession, keep a measured, stately pace—remember, we are not running out of church!

After the procession, know what the custom is in your parish. In some places, the servers stand in a designated place outside while the priest and deacon greet people as they leave. In other places, you simply return to the sacristy.

After Mass

After Mass, servers usually return to the sacristy. Sometimes servers help the sacristan prepare for whatever is happening next—extinguishing the candles, bringing in the books, collecting bulletins. Check with the sacristan after Mass to see if you can help clean up the worship space and put things away in the sacristy. Make yourself useful. When you are ready, hang your alb neatly, buttoning buttons and fastening snaps so that the alb won't wrinkle. Check the schedule or check with the coordinator of your ministry to see when you will serve next.

The chalices and patens vessels used during Mass are purified by a priest, deacon, or instituted acolyte. These appointed ministers will purify the vessels either at the end of the Communion Rite or immediately following Mass. Once these ministers have purified the vessels, servers may assist the sacristan with cleansing. To cleanse vessels, rinse them in the sacrarium. Then thoroughly wash the vessels with soap and warm water, rinse, and dry so they can be used for the next Mass. Used purificators, corporals, and altar cloths should be placed in the designated location for used liturgical linens—usually a special drawer or hamper in the sacristy. The sacristan will take care of cleansing these items later.

Other vessels, like the pitcher and basin for the hand washing, the cruet, and any carafes or pitchers used to hold the wine before it was consecrated, can simply be washed in the sink. You do not need to rinse these items in the sacrarium.

Reverently extinguish all candles. Be sure to use a snuffer so as not to spill wax. Bring to the sacristy all ritual books and vessels.

The ashes from incense and lit coals should also be discarded in a safe place, perhaps buried in the parish garden. Sometimes there is a special metal-lined bin in the sacristy for this purpose. Ask the sacristan or liturgy director about what should happen in your parish.

You can also help to prepare the nave for the next Mass. Pick up discarded bulletins or worship aids so that they can be reused at the next Mass or placed in the vestibule for parishioners to pick up during the week. Gather any lost items—hats, umbrellas, baby toys, etc.—and put them in the designated lost-and-found area, usually in the sacristy or the parish office. Return hymnals and offering envelopes to their holders and raise the kneelers. Throw away any waste, and be attentive to items that can be recycled.

Before you leave the church, don't forget the most important thing: pause for prayer. As Pope John Paul II said to tens of thousands of altar servers who journeyed to Rome in 2001:

> Your service cannot be restricted to the inside of the church.
> It must shine out in your everyday life: at school, in the family,
> and in the different social contexts, for those who want to serve
> Jesus Christ in a church must be his witnesses everywhere . . . .
> Do not hold your candlestick only inside the church but take
> the light of the Gospel to all who live in darkness and are
> going through a difficult time in their lives.[52]

Serving during Other Rites

Sometimes another rite or sacrament will be part of the Sunday Mass, or you might be scheduled to serve at a special rite outside of Sunday Mass or at another scheduled Mass (e.g., a Saturday afternoon or evening wedding). When this is the case, servers will have additional responsibilities.

Rite of Baptism

When infants are baptized, they become part of a new family—the family of faith. As God's adopted children, they become our brothers and sisters in Christ. The celebration of infant Baptisms during the Sunday Mass can renew the whole parish community in our baptismal identity. Servers can help make the celebration of Baptism joyful and memorable both for the families and for the rest of the parish community by being well prepared for the special elements of Mass when the Rite of Baptism is celebrated.

Before Mass begins, make sure everything you need for Mass is prepared, in addition to the special preparations required for the Rite of

Baptism. Assist the sacristan to be sure that the Paschal candle is lit, and that the oils, towels, and candles for the rite are where they need to be. Review procession routes before Mass begins.

The Introductory Rite usually takes place at the back of the church, near the doors, rather than in the sanctuary. Know how this impacts your ministry as a server. Do the cross- and candle-bearers need to gather in a different place than usual? Where are you supposed to stand during the opening dialogue with the parents and godparents? What is your cue to begin the procession toward the sanctuary? Note that an additional server will be needed to hold the ritual book (*Rite of Baptism*) for the celebrant. Notice also that the parents and godparents will usually join the procession to the sanctuary. They walk immediately following the servers and before the readers.

When the ministers reach the sanctuary, Mass continues with the Gloria (except in Advent and Lent) and the Opening Prayer. Notice that the Greeting and the Penitential Rite are omitted.

After the Opening Prayer, Mass proceeds as usual through the homily. After the homily, the intercessions are prayed. Notice that the Creed is not said at this time because a profession of faith will be made with the parents and godparents during the Rite of Baptism.

Following the intercessions, the priest will invite the parents and godparents to bring the child to the baptismal font. Do servers lead the procession to the font? Know the custom in your parish.

At the font, the priest may again need a server to hold the *Rite of Baptism* ritual book. One or two servers may also be needed to assist with the various items that are part of the Rite of Baptism—the sacred chrism, towels, a vessel to pour the water, the white baptismal garment, or the baptismal candle. These items should be placed on a table near the baptismal font before the liturgy begins.

At the font, the priest may pray the prayer of exorcism and anoint the infant with the oil of catechumens (this may also take place at an earlier time, so be aware of the custom in your parish).

Next, the priest will bless the water in the font. He will invite the parents and godparents, with the entire parish community, to renew their baptismal promises. Then the priest baptizes the child, either by immersing him or her in the font or by pouring water over the forehead. Be sure that you are aware of your parish's practice—this will determine how the server assists the priest at this time by holding the vessel (if used) or handing towels to the priest or to the families.

After the Baptism, the priest anoints the infant with sacred chrism. This is the perfumed oil that is consecrated by the Bishop each year at the Chrism Mass. A server may be needed to hold the sacred chrism for the celebrant during the anointings, and another will need to give him a small hand towel (and possibly lemons, depending on local custom) to wipe and clean his hands.

If the infant is not already clothed in a white, baptismal garment, a server may also be needed to bring this garment to the parents or godparents, who will place it on the infant while the priest prays a special prayer. Finally, a server (perhaps the one who held the chrism for the priest) brings the baptismal candle to the father or godfather. Someone from the family—often the father or the godfather—then lights the baptismal candle from the Paschal candle, which (except in the Easter season) stands near the baptismal font. If the Paschal candle is too high, a server may assist by using a candle lighter to bring the flame of the Paschal candle to the smaller baptismal candle.

After the presentation of the baptismal candle the infant, parents, and godparents return to their places in the congregation, and Mass continues as usual with the Preparation of the Altar and of the Gifts. Servers continue with their usual duties to bring the items needed for the Liturgy of the Eucharist.

Note that at the end of the liturgy, there is a special blessing for both the father(s) and mother(s) of those who were baptized. The book-bearer may be needed at this point to hold the ritual book for the priest.

Order of Christian Funerals

When a Christian dies the Church gathers with family members and friends and, through the rituals of the Church, proclaims that through Christ "death no longer has power."[53] Servers assist in the funeral rites. The love and reverence you show in your dignified, well-prepared service at the funeral rites can truly be a comfort to the family, and can help provide the pastoral care that is at the heart of these liturgies.

THE VIGIL: The Vigil is essentially a Liturgy of the Word, similar to the beginning of Mass. There is a Greeting and an Opening Prayer.

Readings from scripture are proclaimed and a psalm is sung. The priest or deacon gives a homily or a lay minister offers a reflection on the readings. There are intercessions, the Lord's Prayer, and a closing prayer. Sometimes family members or friends of the deceased offer a few words of remembrance after the Lord's Prayer.

How servers assist at a vigil depends on the custom in your parish. There may be an Entrance Procession, not unlike Sunday Mass. Servers usually hold the ritual book (*Order of Christian Funerals*) for the celebrant. If candles are used for the proclamation of the Gospel, the candle-bearers will move just as they do for Sunday Mass.[54]

THE FUNERAL MASS: For a funeral Mass (Mass of Christian Burial) the duties of the servers are essentially the same as for Sunday Mass. The main differences occur during the Introductory Rite and the Communion Rite.

The Mass of Christian Burial begins at the doors of the church. The coffin or urn is brought inside the church by the pall bearers. The celebrant and servers meet the family and friends of the deceased for the special prayers that begin the liturgy. The body of the deceased in the coffin is sprinkled with holy water and the pall; a white cloth, which serves as a reminder of Baptism, is draped over the coffin. Servers carry the cross and candles, as usual. An additional server may be needed to hold the ritual text for the celebrant, and to hand the vessel of holy water for the sprinkling of the coffin.[55] A server may also hand the pall to the family, who place it over the coffin.

After the pall is placed, the procession to the sanctuary begins. This procession is much like the Entrance Procession at Sunday Mass, except that the coffin and the family and friends of the deceased will follow the priest. Mass then proceeds as usual until the Prayer after Communion. (You will need to light the coals for the incense at some point during Mass. Perhaps immediately following the proclamation of the Gospel would be a good time to do this.)

After the Prayer after Communion comes a series of special prayers called the Final Commendation. The coffin is incensed and a special Song of Farewell is sung.[56] In this song, the Church commends the deceased Christian to the mercy and care of God.

During the Rite of Commendation, one server may hold the ritual book (*Order of Christian Funerals*) for the celebrant. Another brings the thurible and incense. Meanwhile, the other servers take the cross and candles to stand near the coffin.

The celebrant introduces the Rite of Commendation, and then, during the Song of Farewell, adds incense to the thurible on the coals and walks around the coffin, incensing it in a sign of reverence for the deceased and the dignity of his or her Baptism. The Prayer of Commendation follows, and then the cross-bearer and candle-bearers lead the pallbearers carrying the coffin, and the other ministers to the hearse, in keeping with local custom.

If the funeral takes place outside of Mass, all the rites are as above except that the Lord's Prayer is prayed following the General Intercessions. The liturgy then moves directly to the Final Commendation.

If servers assist at the Rite of Committal in your parish, then usually two will go with the minister to the cemetery. One server holds the ritual book (*Order of Christian Funerals*) for the celebrant and another holds the holy water and sprinkler (if these are used). If the ground has not already been blessed, it is sprinkled with water.

Rite of Marriage

For servers, a wedding Mass is very similar to what you are used to doing at Sunday Mass. The following are some special elements to be aware of. And always keep in mind that customs vary from place to place, and from culture to culture. Be sure you know what the expectations are in your parish.

The Entrance Procession at a wedding, whether it takes place in the context of Mass or the Liturgy of the Word, may be led by a cross and candles, carried by servers. Sometimes, there is a formal seating of some members of the family before the liturgical procession begins. Notice that in the procession itself, the wedding party—bridesmaids, groomsmen, witnesses, and the bride and groom and their parents—follows the celebrant. After the procession, the priest welcomes all present. There may be a Penitential Act, although this may also be omitted. Then the server holds the book for the Opening Prayer and all are seated for the Liturgy of the Word—just like at Sunday Mass.

After the homily, the priest (or deacon) goes to the bride and groom, who usually stand before the altar for the Rite of Marriage. One

NOTE: Under the heading *Sunday Celebrations in the Absence of a Priest,* the first sentence in the second paragraph should read, "*Sunday Celebrations in the Absence of a Priest* is not Mass."

Serving the Liturgy **63**

server will need to hold the ritual book for the celebrant, for the blessing of rings, which takes place immediately following the exchange of consent.[57]

An additional server may be needed to carry a small tray on which the best man will place the rings for the blessing. Be sure to check with the celebrant or liturgist for any special details about this part of the wedding Mass.

After the exchange of rings, the General Intercessions (Prayer of the Faithful) will be prayed. A server may be needed to hold the book for the celebrant as he gives the introduction to the intercessions. When a wedding is celebrated in the context of the Liturgy of the Word, a special prayer of blessing called the Nuptial Blessing is now prayed over the couple. If the wedding takes place in the context of Mass, the Liturgy of the Eucharist proceeds as usual, with the Preparation of the Altar and of the Gifts and the reception of the gifts. At a wedding Mass, the Nuptial Blessing takes place immediately following the Lord's Prayer.

In some places, a cross and candles leads the newly married couple out of the church; in other places, they lead the procession themselves. Parish custom will provide direction for many details for wedding liturgies.

Sunday Celebrations in the Absence of a Priest

In some parishes, a priest is not available to celebrate Mass regularly on Sundays. Because it is so essential for Christians to gather on Sunday, the Church has provided a ritual for deacons or lay persons called Sunday Celebrations in the Absence of a Priest. The ritual enables a deacon or lay person to preside over the Sunday worship of the community in parishes or missions without a priest. This service takes the form of a Liturgy of the Word or the Liturgy of the Hours, followed by the distribution of Holy Communion.

Sunday Celebrations in the Absence of a Priest is Mass. The celebrant's chair is not used. There is no Eucharistic Prayer. No gifts are presented. Servers do not wash the celebrant's hands, nor will bells be rung. And Holy Communion is distributed from the hosts reserved in the tabernacle and previously consecrated at Mass by the priest.

Still, servers who assist at these liturgies will continue to do some things that are similar to their duties during Mass. They carry the cross and candles to lead the processions, and they assist by holding the ritual book for the celebrant. And of course they serve as models of full and engaged participation in the prayer of the community.

When the Bishop Is Present

Sometimes the Bishop of your diocese will come to the parish to celebrate Mass and other sacraments. This is a joyous occasion for the parish, for the Bishop is a sign of unity in the local Church, and stands as witness to the faith that we have received from the apostles. The Bishop often comes for the installation of a new pastor or for a milestone anniversary in a parish community, like a centennial. But most often, the Bishop comes to celebrate the Rite of Confirmation during Mass.

When the Bishop comes, *at least* two additional servers are needed—this will vary from diocese to diocese. One serves as crosier-bearer, to care for the Bishop's pastoral staff. The other serves as miter-bearer, taking care of the special hat the Bishop wears at various times during the Mass. These two servers, along with the others, will usually be directed by the Bishop's Master of Ceremonies during the Mass.[58] Here is a simple outline of the Mass for crosier-bearers and miter-bearers:

Entrance Procession	Bishop wears miter, carries crosier
At foot of altar	Bishop hands miter and crosier to servers before reverencing altar
After Opening Prayer	Bishop puts miter back on for readings
At Alleluia	Bishop blesses deacon who will read Gospel, then stands and takes off miter and receives crosier
During Gospel	Bishop stands, without miter, holding the crosier
During Homily	Bishop may use both miter and crosier during homily, which may be given either from his chair or from the ambo; or he may use neither
After Homily	If he wore the miter and/or used the crosier during the homily, the Bishop takes them off for the Creed and Prayer of the Faithful

After Intercessions	Bishop receives miter and sits as the altar is prepared and gifts are received
Preparation of Gifts	Bishop takes off miter before he goes to the altar
After the Prayer over the Gifts	Before the Preface Dialogue, the Bishop's zucchetto (skullcap) is removed
After Communion	The Bishop puts his zucchetto back on as he returns to his place following Holy Communion
Greeting	The Bishop puts his miter back on before the greeting ("The Lord be with you")
Blessing	Before the Blessing, the Bishop receives his crosier. He wears the miter and carries the crosier in the procession out of the church.

RITE OF CONFIRMATION: In most dioceses, the Bishop comes to the parish at least once a year, often to celebrate the sacrament of Confirmation. Here are some elements of this rite to keep in mind. After the Gospel, the pastor presents to the Bishop the candidates for Confirmation. The Bishop then gives the homily, speaking directly to the candidates.

After the homily, the Bishop invites the candidates for Confirmation to renew their baptismal promises. A server will probably be needed to hold the special ritual text. The Bishop may carry out the rite from his chair, or he may come to a special place before the altar or at the head of the main aisle. Those to be confirmed come forward for the sacrament. A server may be needed to stand next to the Bishop, holding a vessel with the sacred chrism.

After the candidates have been anointed, the server holding the chrism takes the vessel to the credence table as the Bishop goes back to the presidential chair. The Bishop will need to wash his hands. Two servers may assist with this, bringing from the credence table a pitcher, basin, and towel. In some parishes, the servers bring a sliced lemon as well, which helps to take the oil off the Bishop's hands. After the Bishop's hands have been washed, the Mass continues as usual.

The Liturgical Year

The Catholic Church observes a rich and varied calendar of seasons and special days, and a good server will be familiar with them.

✠ Christ's saving work is celebrated in sacred memory by the Church on fixed days throughout the year. Each week on the day called the Lord's Day the Church commemorates the Lord's resurrection. Once a year at Easter the Church honors this resurrection and passion with the utmost solemnity. In fact through the yearly cycle the Church unfolds the entire mystery of Christ and keeps the anniversaries of the saints.

—General Norms for the Liturgical Year and the Calendar, 1

Sunday is our principal feast day; it is the anchor of the liturgical year. It is the Lord's Day, the day on which Jesus rose from the dead. Gathering on Sunday, week after week, we commemorate the Resurrection of Christ. In that sense, every Sunday is a celebration of Easter.

Other liturgical days are grouped in order of their significance. **Solemnities** are the principal days in the calendar, such as Easter, Christmas, the Epiphany of the Lord, the Ascension of the Lord, and Pentecost. Other solemnities include the days honoring the Nativity of Saint John the Baptist (June 24), the martyrdoms of Saint Peter and Saint Paul (June 29), and the Immaculate Conception of the Blessed Virgin Mary (December 8). The principal patrons of the parish, as well as the church's anniversary of dedication, are also celebrated as solemnities.

Feasts take the next rank. Some feasts honor events in the life of Christ, such as the Presentation of the Lord (February 2) and the Transfiguration of the Lord (August 6). Others recall Mary and the apostles and evangelists, like the feast of Our Lady of Guadalupe (December 12), the feast of Saint Matthew (September 21), or the feast of the Conversion of Saint Paul (January 25). Some feasts honor the mysteries of our faith, like the Feast of the Exaltation of the Holy Cross (September 14) and the Feast of the Most Holy Trinity (Sunday after Pentecost).

Memorials are the next in the rank of holy days. They call to mind saints who have influenced the universal Church, like Saint Mary Magdalene (July 22), Saint Thomas Aquinas (January 28), Saint Augustine (August 28), or Saint Thérèse of Lisieux (October 1).

Optional memorials come next. Local churches may choose whether or not to observe them. Some saints whose memorials are optional include Saint Romuald (June 19), Saint Elizabeth of Portugal (July 4), and Saint Louis (August 25).

All other days are simply called "weekdays," no matter when they fall.

The liturgical year does not begin on January 1. Instead, it begins with the season of **Advent**, which starts on the fourth Sunday before Christmas. Advent is a season of preparation and anticipation, as we look to the Second Coming of Christ and prepare to celebrate the solemnity of his birth. From Advent, we move into the season of **Christmas**, which overflows from Christmas Eve to a whole liturgical season in which we recall the coming of Christ in human flesh. The Christmas season includes the feast of the Holy Family of Jesus, Mary, and Joseph, the solemnity of the Epiphany of the Lord, and ends on the feast of the Baptism of the Lord.

The season of **Lent** begins on Ash Wednesday. It is a season of intense prayer in preparation for Easter. Lent is especially associated with fasting and almsgiving, and with special devotions like the Stations of the Cross. Lent prepares us for Holy Week, which begins on Palm Sunday, and especially for the Paschal Triduum, the three days leading up to Easter. The **Paschal Triduum** is the shortest liturgical season of the year, and the most important. On Holy Thursday, Good Friday, Holy Saturday, and Easter Sunday, we are renewed each year in what it means to be a Christian. **Easter** Sunday marks the beginning of a new liturgical season, and for 50 days we continue to celebrate the Resurrection of the Lord. The Easter Season concludes with Pentecost, when we celebrate the coming of the Holy Spirit into the Church.

The rest of the liturgical year is called Ordinary Time. The word *ordinary* in this case does not mean "normal" or "boring"; rather, it comes from a Latin word meaning "numbered." The season of Ordinary Time is the longest season of the liturgical year. It begins following Christmas, and is interrupted by Lent and Easter, resuming after the solemnity of Pentecost and continuing until the end of the liturgical year. The last Sunday of the year is the solemnity of Our Lord Jesus Christ the King. Then a new liturgical year begins with the First Sunday of Advent.

Through the liturgical year, we proclaim Christ as the Lord of all times and seasons.[59] Here is a simple outline, which provides the proper colors, the dates of celebration, and a quick explanation of the seasons.[60]

Advent

Color	Violet (Rose may be worn on the Third Sunday)
Time	Begins four Sundays before Christmas and ends after mid-afternoon prayer on Christmas Eve
Meaning	Waiting in joyful hope for the coming of Christ. It is a season both to prepare for Christmas when Christ's First Coming is remembered and to direct our minds to his Second Coming at the end of time.

Christmas

Color	White (and gold/silver)
Time	Begins with Evening Prayer on Christmas Eve and ends with Evening Prayer on the feast of the Baptism of the Lord.
Meaning	We celebrate God's gift of love in the Incarnation of his Son, Jesus Christ. We celebrate God's covenant, his promises, and we ponder his mysterious presence among his people. It is a season of light.

Ordinary Time

Color	Green
Time	Begins after Evening Prayer on the feast of the Baptism of the Lord and continues until Ash Wednesday. Season continues after Evening Prayer on the solemnity of Pentecost and continues until before Evening Prayer I on the First Sunday of Advent.

Meaning	This is counted time; each Sunday has a unique consecutive number. This season focuses not on particular aspects of the Paschal Mystery but Christ in his fullness.

Lent

Color	Violet (Rose may be worn on Fourth Sunday)
Time	Begins on Ash Wednesday and continues until the Evening Mass of the Lord's Supper on Holy Thursday.
Meaning	Penitential season of prayer, fasting, and almsgiving, which prepares the elect for the reception of Baptism, and the baptized for the renewal of baptismal promises at Easter.

Paschal Triduum

Color	White (Red on Good Friday)
Time	Begins with the Evening Mass of the Lord's Supper on Holy Thursday and concludes with Evening Prayer on Easter Sunday.
Meaning	The climax of the liturgical year— celebrating the Passion, death, and Resurrection of Christ, the Paschal Mystery.

Easter

Color	White (Gold/Silver; Red on Pentecost)
Time	Begins on Easter Sunday and concludes with Evening Prayer on the solemnity of Pentecost.
Meaning	Fifty days of feasting and celebration of Christ's rising from the dead, his ascension into heaven, and the sending of his Holy Spirit.

Servers should also be aware of the following colors for solemnities, feasts, and memorials.

Solemnities:	White (usually)
Feasts of the Lord:	White
Feasts of Apostles:	Red (usually)
Feasts of Saints (not martyrs):	White
Feasts of Mary:	White
Memorials of Mary:	White
Memorials of Saints:	White
Memorials of Martyrs:	Red

In some cases, the colors as noted above will vary. For example, although feasts of the Lord are typically white, the feast of the Exaltation of the Holy Cross is red. All Souls' Day is also a rather unusual day. It is ranked as a "commemoration" rather than a solemnity, feast, or memorial. Violet, black, or white may be used on this day. When confused, it is always best to consult your local Ordo or ask the presiding priest or liturgist.

The Master of Ceremonies

The master of ceremonies (MC) is a server with many years of experience in liturgical ministry. It is a demanding, yet rewarding, role. To be an MC you need to know the ins and outs of all that a server does, and be familiar with all the details and rubrics of the Mass and the full range of rites and celebrations. The MC is responsible for the proper conduct

and flow of the liturgy, ensuring that each minister is where he or she needs to be, and that each element of the liturgy happens smoothly and without distracting or disruptive pauses or confusions.

Certain complex liturgies, like the liturgies of the Paschal Triduum, may require a rehearsal. The MC will often work with the liturgical coordinator at the rehearsal to help the other servers learn their part in the liturgy.

An MC will often serve when the Bishop is present.

To be an MC, you should be well organized and have the ability to work with other liturgical ministers before, during, and after the liturgy. A good MC can take charge in a positive and friendly manner.

Qualities of a Server Ministry Director

The best director for the server ministry is an adult who loves to serve. Like the master of ceremonies, the director of the server ministry must have an excellent understanding of Mass. He or she must also be organized and be able to work effectively with young people. If you are interested in helping to direct altar servers, you should have the following qualities:

LEADER: You will need to get to know each altar server, providing guidance, tracking their capabilities, and ensuring that each server continues to learn new things. With young servers (and sometimes with older ones) conflicts or a sense of competition can arise. Your calm presence, and your words of wisdom, can make the experience of serving a positive and prayerful one for everyone.

MENTOR: You must be willing to take the time to patiently teach by word and, even more, by example. Your words and actions should convey your love for the Church's liturgy and your care for each server's development.

COORDINATOR: You will need to schedule servers for Sunday Mass and for a variety of other liturgies, and assign server duties based on each server's experience and the demands of the liturgy. You will need to be able to handle last-minute changes and offer resolutions for scheduling conflicts and the needs of the servers.

The Adult Server as Mentor

Adult servers will almost automatically find themselves in the role of mentor, especially if you serve alongside children or teenagers. For some, this may be a daunting prospect, especially if you have had limited experience working with children and youth. Yet, helping younger servers is an important aspect of this liturgical ministry. You are a mentor when you help children and teens recognize that that they are an important part of the parish community. You are a mentor when you help

Helping younger servers is an important part of your liturgical ministry.

young people realize that they have talents and gifts to offer for the glory of God and the good of others. You are a mentor when you help young people to experience the liturgy as the source and summit of the Christian life. Here are a few tips as you begin:

1. **A mentor is a model.** Children and teenagers will often be more influenced by what you do than what you say; they will look to you as a guide simply because you are an adult. So be a model of good service: arrive early so you can receive instruction and prepare for Mass; participate fully in Mass by listening, singing, responding, and praying; be available after Mass to assist others with clean up and to tighten loose ends.

2. **A mentor is a person of prayer and service.** As a mentor, ask for God's guidance in your ministry, and take time before and after Mass to thank God for his gifts and blessings. Live the call of the liturgy by sharing the love of Christ with others, not just on Sunday but throughout the week.

3. **A mentor is genuine.** Know yourself—your weaknesses as well as your strengths. The more honest you are with yourself, the better able you will be to appreciate other people's talents and to deal with their mistakes with understanding and compassion. Children, especially teens, who are in the process of developing, maturing, and seeking to define themselves, will intuitively pick up on your confidence and compassion and will learn about the love and acceptance that God offers his children.

4. **A mentor is open to learning and growing.** Appreciate the gifts that children and teenagers offer, their sense of wonder and awe about God and the Church, their excitement about participating in the liturgy as altar servers. Even the youngest

people among us can teach us important things about our relationship with God and our role as a liturgical minister.

5. **A mentor gives genuine encouragement.** As you come to know the gifts and skills of the youth you are working with, be sure to offer praise for a job well done and provide guidance to servers who are new or who lack confidence.

6. **Mentors share their experience with others.** While not everyone that you serve with will look to you as a guide, never underestimate your example of prayer and faithfulness to God. When the opportunity presents itself, share why you feel called to this ministry and, more importantly, share why you feel it is important to attend Mass. In doing so, you will help children and teenagers begin to articulate their own relationship with God and the Church. Serving at the liturgy will, hopefully, mark the beginning of a life committed to worship, prayer, and service.

7. **A mentor is not a disciplinarian.** While there may be times when you will need to remind young servers of appropriate behavior, your main role is to model participation in the liturgy, not to discipline. If you do encounter problems with younger servers, inform the ministry director, who can step in when intervention is needed.

8. **A mentor is not a friend.** Appropriate boundaries are necessary to keep relationships between adults and children or teenagers healthy and safe. For your safety as well as theirs, you should not be alone with children. Ask the coordinator of your ministry about guidelines for ministry for adults who work with children. Most dioceses have excellent programs available to keep you and the young people safe.[61]

PROTECTING GOD'S CHILDREN: If you will be working directly with children, check with your parish administrator to see if the parish or diocese requires older ministers to participate in specialized training that will safeguard the protection of youth. VIRTUS ® is a brand name for best practices programs designed by the National Catholic Risk

Retention Group, Inc. to support churches and religious institutions in preventing child sexual abuse. The "Protecting God's Children" program is for the education of employees, volunteers, and parents in parishes, Catholic schools and diocesan offices. All parish personnel who work with children (paid or volunteer) should be certified through this program or a similar program. These excellent programs will help you to be more aware of what kinds of behavior are inappropriate, and it will help you to recognize the signs of abuse. By participating in these programs you can truly help to prevent child sexual abuse in the Church.[62]

Questions for Discussion and Reflection

1. How would you define service? What does this mean in relationship to the Christian community?

_____

_____

_____

_____

2. What do you think it means to serve the liturgy? Do you serve in other ways outside the liturgy? What are these service opportunities?

_____

_____

_____

_____

3. Do you feel prepared to serve your community? Do you understand your responsibilities, the parts of the Mass, and other rites?

_____

_____

_____

_____

NOTES

1. Adapted from *The Liturgical Ministry Series: Guide for Ministers of the Liturgical Environment* by Paul Turner and Mary Pat Storms.

2. *Rite of Dedication of a Church* (RDC), 1.

3. 1 Peter 2:9.

4. *Built of Living Stones* (BLS), 54.

5. *Rite of Dedication of an Altar* (RDA), 4.

6. RDA, 48.

7. BLS, 61.

8. CSL, 51.

9. GIRM, 310.

10. An action reserved to priests, deacons, and instituted acolytes.

11. GIRM, 316.

12. BLS, 67; referencing Congregation for Divine Worship, *Rite of Christian Initiation of Adults*, 213: "Therefore in the celebration of baptism the washing with water should take on its full importance as the sign of that mystical sharing in Christ's death and resurrection through which those who believe in his name die to sin and rise to eternal life. Either immersion or the pouring of water should be chosen for the rite, whichever will serve in individual cases and in the various traditions and circumstances to ensure the clear understanding that this washing is not a mere purification rite but the sacrament of being joined to Christ."

13. *Rite of Baptism* (RB), 60.

14. The Sacramentary.

15. The Paschal candle is placed near the ambo during the Easter season.

16. *Rite of Penance*, 46.

17. See page 66 for additional information regarding the liturgical year.

18. RB, 99.

19. See Luke 4:16–21.

20. Please see page 47 for processional instructions, and page 45 for placement instructions.

21. See Exodus 25:31.

22. Revelation 1:12.

23. RDC, 71.

24. A. G. Martimort. *The Church at Prayer: Liturgy and Time.* Collegeville, MN: The Liturgical Press, 1986, p. 198.

25. See Luke 1: 8–11.

26. See Matthew 2:11.

27. See Revelation 8:3b.

28. GIRM, 276.

29. BLS, 236–237.

30. GIRM, 109.

31. See CSL, 10.

32. Ibid.

33. See page 78 for additional information.

34. Because setup primarily falls under the responsibilities of the sacristan, items that directly involve the server are only addressed here. A more detailed description of Mass setup is included in *The Liturgical Ministry Series: Guide for Sacristans* by Corinna Laughlin and Paul Turner. Refer also to LTP's free downloadable sacristan check list: www.LTP.org.

35. See GIRM, 118.

36. CSL, 14.

37. 1 Corinthians 12:5.

38. Please see page 70 for more information regarding the master of ceremonies.

39. See GIRM, 120, 173, 277, 49, 123, 276b.

40. The Gloria is not sung or said on the Sundays of Advent or Lent.

41. On Sundays during Advent or Lent, the Opening Prayer follows the Penitential Act.

42. The Sacramentary.

43. Ibid.

44. Ibid.

45. Ibid.

46. Ibid.

47. See GIRM, 150.

48. The Sacramentary.

49. Ibid.

50. Ibid.

51. Ibid.

52. General Audience of Wednesday, August 1, 2001; available from http://www. vaticanva/holy _father/john_paul_ii/audiences/2001/documents/hf_jp-ii_aud _20010801_en.html.

53. Romans 6:9.

54. If it happens that your parish sometimes wakes the deceased *in the church* before the funeral, then servers may be needed for the Reception of the Body. In this case the ritual is a Liturgy of the Word, which begins with the reception of the body. The Reception of the Body takes place exactly as it does as it is described above for the Mass of Christian Burial: The celebrant and servers meet the family and friends of the deceased for the special prayers that begin the liturgy. The body of the deceased in the coffin is sprinkled with holy water, and the pall is draped over the coffin.

55. In some parish churches, the baptismal font is located by the entryway. In these churches, an additional vessel of water is not necessary; the water used for sprinkling the coffin is taken directly from the baptismal font.

56. The coffin is sprinkled if the sprinkling did not occur during the Introductory Rite. Servers may assist.

57. If your parish blesses the rings with holy water, another server will need to hold the holy water and sprinkler for this part of the rite.

58. See page 70.

59. The above section on the liturgical year was adapted from *Guide for Sacristans* (LTP, 2008) by Paul Turner.

60. Outline provided by Robert D. Shadduck.

61. The "Server as Mentor" was written by Latisse Heerwig.

62. VIRTUS® offers suggestions about how to keep some of these boundaries clear. See www.virtus.org for more information.

Frequently Asked Questions

1. Do I need to worry about what I am wearing underneath the alb?

If an alb (or, as in some parishes, a cassock) is worn over clothing, you can wear regular street attire. However, make sure that your collar, sleeves, and pant legs do not show.

Be careful not to wear clothing in which logos or images will show through the alb.

You should be conscious of what kind of shoes you are wearing so your walking from one location to another is not a distraction. Avoid wearing squeaky shoes, those that have smooth bottoms (so not to slip!), or shoes with harder bottoms (they would be loud when walking from one place to another). It is best not to wear high heels, sandals, flip-flops, or clunky sneakers. You might consider wearing soft flats or loafers in black or brown.

You should meet with the liturgical ministry coordinator and try on various albs (or cassocks) to find the correct size. The alb should be ankle length. For safety reasons, it is important that your alb doesn't drag on the floor. Albs that are too short or too long are not attractive for public prayer. The sleeves should rest slightly above the wrist. Long sleeves will only be distracting and present a safety risk because you will probably be working with candles.

2. Where should I sit during Mass?

Where to sit will depend upon the layout of your worship space and your assigned responsibilities. A good rule of thumb is to sit as close as possible to where you will be performing your liturgical function so that your duties will not cause distraction and can be enacted smoothly and transparently. Depending on your assigned responsibilities, you should sit in designated areas near the presidential chair, credence table, or even the ambo. For example, if you will be holding the Roman Missal (Sacramentary) for the priest celebrant during the Opening Prayer, you will want to sit in a place that is between where the book is placed and the presidential chair. In this way, you can turn discreetly to retrieve the book, walk toward the priest celebrant (if walking is needed), and open the book, holding it as you have been instructed. You should not be crossing back and forth, nor should you need a significant amount of time to bring the book to the priest celebrant. Your pastor, liturgist, or liturgical ministry coordinator should tell you where to sit. If you are confused, be sure to consult with them *before* Mass begins.

3. How should I sit?

The answer to this question may seem obvious; however, it is always good to remember that although you may not be *doing* something (i.e., one of your assigned responsibilities), you are still in a public forum for prayer and are a model for the rest of the assembly. Be attentive to what is going on. Respond. Sing. Be silent. Sit down carefully. Sit tall with both feet on the floor. Never slouch or seem uninterested. Keep your hands folded or laid flat on your lap. Pray!

4. Is there a certain way I should walk when preparing things during Mass?

Keep your back straight, but relaxed in a way so as not to appear stiff. Walk slowly, smoothly, and gracefully. The pace is deliberate, but not rushed. When walking with other servers, walk together in a unified motion. Keep your hands folded when you are not carrying vessels or other items.

5. How should I stand during Mass?

Servers should always stand up straight with both feet firmly on the floor. Your feet should be about six to eight inches apart. This will give you balance and comfort. Never stand with your knees locked. Standing too long in this manner could actually cause fainting. Keep your hands folded when you are not carrying vessels or other items.

6. Is there a certain way I should bow?

The manner in which you bow is dependent upon who or what you are bowing to. A bow signifies reverence and honor. There are two types of bows: a bow of the head and a profound bow. To make a profound bow, bend at the waist. The bow of the head is simply that—only the head is bent forward. All bows should have a smooth and slow forward incline.

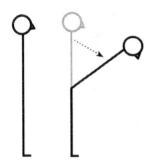

A profound bow is made when crossing in front of the altar and during the Creed at the words *by the power of the Holy Spirit . . . became man.* When receiving Holy Communion, you should bow your head before the sacrament as a gesture of reverence just before receiving the Body and Blood of the Lord.

7. *If the tabernacle is in the sanctuary, do you genuflect before the reserved sacrament during the Mass?*

No. When the tabernacle is located in the sanctuary, the priest and other ministers genuflect when they approach the altar (during the Entrance

Procession) and when they depart (closing procession), "but not during the celebration of the Mass itself."[1] If the server is a candle-bearer, cross-bearer, or thurifer during these processions, they do not genuflect; rather, they give a slight bow of the head before the altar. During the Mass, if you cross before the altar, "a deep bow is made to the altar."[2, 3]

8. *How should I walk down steps?*

A server should never back down steps in the sanctuary. This is important for safety reasons. You can also lift your alb slightly when walking down the steps so you do not trip.

9. *What should I do if something unexpected happens?*

No matter how well you have prepared to serve, sometimes things go wrong. Candles could blow out; books could fall; coals might burn out; you might stumble; etc. When something goes wrong, stay calm. When a problem arises, think about it for a moment and then do what is required to correct the problem in a way that is not distracting to other ministers or to the assembly.

10. *Where should I focus my attention during the liturgy?*

A server should always look toward the focal point—the place where the action is taking place. This could be any of the following: presidential chair, ambo, altar, or the baptismal font. When moving from place to place, it is best for you to look straight ahead—toward where you are going. Staring or looking around at other persons or things can unnecessarily distract the assembly. Remember to be attentive to the prayers and readings. Respond, sing, pray, and observe silence and proper gestures.

> *11. I was an altar server when I was a child. I remember ringing bells during the consecration. Now, this isn't the practice in my parish, yet it is in a parish nearby. Why do some churches still ring bells and others do not?*

This will actually vary from parish to parish. The ringing of bells is optional. "A little before the consecration, when appropriate, a server rings a bell as a signal to the faithful. According to local custom, the server also rings the bell as the priest shows the host and then the chalice."[4]

> *12. What does it mean to "purify" the sacred vessels? Is that different from cleaning the vessels after Mass?*

The vessels that contain the consecrated bread and wine during the Mass receive a special cleansing called "purification" following Holy Communion or immediately following Mass. This purification stems from our Catholic belief in the real presence of Christ in Eucharist, and it is carried out to ensure that any particles of the sacred species that may have remained in the paten or the chalice are reverently consumed. This rite of purification is carried out by a priest, deacon, or instituted acolyte.

Following Holy Communion, or following Mass, usually at the credence table, the paten and ciboria are carefully wiped over a chalice, so that any crumbs or fragments that remain can be collected. Any remaining Precious Blood is consumed, and then the chalices are rinsed with water (or with a mixture of wine and water, according to local custom), which the minister then consumes.

After this rite of purification, the vessels are ready to be cleaned by the sacristan or another minister: they are carefully rinsed in the sacrarium, and then washed and dried in the usual way.[5]

13. In my parish, I serve during the early morning Mass, but I also sing in the contemporary ensemble for the 11:00 Mass. May I receive Holy Communion at both Masses?

Yes! You may receive Holy Communion, provided you participate fully in each liturgy.

14. We don't always use the Book of the Gospels in the Entrance Procession. When we don't, I'm instructed to place it on the altar before Mass. Is there a proper way to display it upon the altar?

The Book of the Gospels is often richly decorated and very expensive. We reverence the Book of the Gospels by carrying it in procession, placing it on the altar, and processing it to the ambo for the proclamation of the Gospel. It is not necessary or advisable to give reverence to the book by standing it up, open, on the altar. Over time, this will pull the pages out of the binding and ruin a book that should last the church several generations. It is acceptable to simply lay the book flat on the altar.[6]

15. What is the Roman Missal? Is that different from the Sacramentary?

In the early years of the Church, several different books were used for the celebration of the Mass—a Sacramentary that included the priest's prayers, a Lectionary that included the readings, an Evangelary or Book of the Gospels containing just the readings of the Gospel. Later on, books began to be prepared that were complete in themselves. This kind of book was known as a *"Missale Plenum,"* that is, "complete missal" (the Latin *missalis* means "having to do with the Mass"). From the time of the Council of Trent, there was one book that contained both the readings and the prayers for the Mass, called the *Missale Romanum.*

Following the Second Vatican Council, with the vast expansion of the readings used at the liturgy, one-volume editions became impractical, and the tradition of separate Sacramentaries and Lectionaries was restored. However, the term "Missal Romanum" is still used to describe the Latin edition of what we call the "Sacramentary." When the English translation of the revised GIRM appeared in 2002, the term "Roman Missal" was used throughout. So the term "Roman Missal" is used in this *Guide for Servers.*

Although the terms can be confusing, both "Roman Missal" and "Sacramentary" refer to the same book containing the prayers used by the priest for the Mass of the Roman rite.[7]

NOTES

1. GIRM, 274.

2. *Ceremonial of Bishops*, 72.

3. Adapted from Virginia Meagher's "Frequently Asked Questions," as originally published in *The Liturgical Ministry Series: Guide for Lectors* (LTP, 2007).

4. GIRM, 150.

5. See GIRM, 278–280. This question was written by Corinna Laughlin as originally published in *The Liturgical Ministry Series: Guide for Sacristans* (LTP, 2008).

6. Written by Corinna Laughlin, as originally published in *The Liturgical Ministry Series: Guide for Sacristans* (LTP, 2008).

7. Written by Corinna Laughlin, as originally published in *The Liturgical Ministry Series: Guide for Sacristans* (LTP, 2008).

Resources

Liturgical Documents

Built of Living Stones: Art, Architecture, and Worship (BLS). This document from the United States Conference of Catholic Bishops is intended primarily as a guide to building or renovating churches, but it is useful for all who are involved in the liturgy or in the maintenance of a church building. It is available in LTP's *Liturgy Documents, Volume One.*

Ceremonial of Bishops. This instructional document details how liturgy is to be celebrated with the Bishop. The full text is available from The Liturgical Press. Excerpts of the document are found in LTP's *Liturgy Documents, Volume One.*

Constitution on the Sacred Liturgy (CSL). The first constitution promulgated from the Second Vatican Council, this document forms the basis for our communal worship and includes sections on the participation of the assembly, liturgical inculturation, the Liturgy of the Hours, the liturgical year, and sacred music and art. It is available in LTP's *Liturgy Documents, Volume One.*

Eucharistic Documents for the New Millennium: Documentos Eucaristicos para el Nuevo Milenio. Chicago, IL: Liturgy Training Publications, 2004. A bilingual companion to the *General Instruction of the Roman Missal,* containing documents in both English and Spanish that will greatly assist faith communities prepare for and evaluate the community's celebration of the Lord's Day Eucharist. The included *Redemptionis Sacramentum* is of particular concern for servers since it deals with instructions for the celebration of Mass.

General Instruction of the Roman Missal (GIRM). This document deals specifically with the celebration of Mass. It is the primary reference document for discovering the hows and whys of almost any aspect of Eucharistic liturgy. It is available in LTP's *Liturgy Documents, Volume One.*

The Liturgy Documents, Volume One: A Parish Resource (Fourth Edition). Chicago, IL: Liturgy Training Publications, 2004. A key resource of Church documents on the liturgy that belongs in every parish resource library.

Liturgy Documents, Volume Two. Chicago, IL: Liturgy Training Publications, 1999. More Vatican and conference documents with a very helpful topical index for both volumes of this resource.

Paschale Solemnitatis: On Preparing and Celebrating the Paschal Feasts. This document concerns how to properly celebrate the liturgies of Lent, Triduum, and Easter. It is available in LTP's *Liturgy Documents, Volume Two.*

Pastoral Resources

Johnson, Lawrence J. *The Mystery of Faith: A Study of the Structural Elements of the Order of the Mass (revised edition).* The Federation of Diocesan Liturgical Commissions, 1999. This is an accessible guide to Mass. It traces the history of Mass and provides a theological overview of each element with supporting documentation.

Laughlin, Corinna, and Paul Turner. *The Liturgical Ministry Series: Guide for Sacristans.* Chicago, IL: Liturgy Training Publications, 2008. Although geared toward sacristans, this training resource provides detailed information concerning the sacristy, layout of churches, set up and clean up for Mass and other rites, which the server will also find helpful.

Philippart, David. *Serve God with Gladness: A Manual for Servers.* Chicago, IL: Liturgy Training Publications, 1998. This book is for teaching children how to serve Mass and other rites. In true workbook style, many pages have sections to fill in and activities to do. Information and guidelines from the adults who work with servers can be noted in specific areas. Artwork, photographs, and diagrams illustrate actions and movement clearly. Vocabulary words are indicated in bold type, and their definitions can be found in the glossary in the back of the book.

Ryan, G. Thomas. *The Sacristy Manual.* Chicago, IL: Liturgy Training Publications, 1993. This book is a wonderful resource, a cornucopia of liturgical information. The first section focuses on preparing to celebrate our liturgies. The manual provides detailed information from the layout of the sanctuary to each of the items used during our celebrations. There are checklists at the end of the manual. The first checklist outlines what is needed for the celebration of Eucharist, and then numeral checklists are provided for the liturgical seasons and important feasts and solemnities.

Turner, Paul. *A Guide to the General Instruction of the Roman Missal.* Chicago, IL: Liturgy Training Publications, 2003. A brief, handy, and straightforward commentary on the *General Instruction of the Roman Missal* for ordained and lay ecclesial ministers. Turner highlights three important principles: the sacrifice of Christ, the holiness of Eucharist, and the participation of the ministers.

Annual Publications and Periodicals

Daily Prayer. Chicago, IL: Liturgy Training Publications. A must-have prayer resource for all liturgical ministers. Using a familiar order of prayer (psalmody, scripture, brief reflection, Prayer of the Faithful, Lord's Prayer, and closing prayer), this annual publication is ideal for personal and communal reflection upon the word of God. The portable size of this book makes it convenient to carry in a purse, briefcase, or backpack, and it provides an easy way to get into the habit of daily prayer that is in sync with the liturgical year.

Ordo (The Order of Prayer in the Liturgy of the Hours and Celebration of the Eucharist). Published by Paulist Press for the various dioceses archdioceses within the United States, this is the resource of choice to be consulted when setting up for the liturgy of the day.

Pastoral Liturgy®. Chicago, IL: Liturgy Training Publications. This is the liturgy magazine for the whole parish. Previously known as *Rite* Magazine, this journal is published six times a year. The contents are tailored to the forthcoming liturgical season with feature articles and those that focus on liturgical ministries and liturgical catechesis.

Sourcebook for Sundays, Seasons, and Weekdays: The Almanac for Pastoral Liturgy. Chicago, IL: Liturgy Training Publications. This publication provides commentary on the readings of the year, as well as plenty of background information on the seasons, solemnities, feasts, and memorials with suggestions on how to prepare for them. It is an excellent resource to use in conjunction with your local Ordo. Visit www.Liturgy Sourcebook.org for a **free** download of additional resources for all aspects of liturgy. Originally published in *Sourcebook for Sundays, Seasons, and Weekdays*, this list is updated each year and is available as a PDF.

Glossary

ALB: A long, white garment worn by priests, deacons, and lay ministers. It is a reminder of the white garment given in Baptism.

ALTAR: A dignified and stationary place from where the sacrifice of our Lord is offered to the Father and made present to us. It represents Christ. It is the focal point for the Liturgy of the Eucharist. The altar is the table from where we receive Christ in his body and blood.

ALTAR CLOTH: Large, white cloth covering the altar.

AMBO: A dignified and stationary place from which the readings, Responsorial Psalm, and *Exsultet* are to be proclaimed. It may also be used for giving the homily and for announcing the intentions of the Prayer of the Faithful. It is the focal point for the Liturgy of the Word.*

AMBRY: Repository for the oil of catechumens, oil of the sick, and sacred chrism.

AMICE: A square, white cloth, which is tied around the neck to cover the collar; used when the alb does not cover the collar completely.

ASPERGILLUM: An instrument used for the sprinkling of holy water; a live branch can also be used as an aspergillum.

BAPTISTRY: The place in the church building where the font for Baptism is located.

BENEDICTION: A blessing given by a priest with the Blessed Sacrament exposed in a monstrance.

BOAT: A small container that holds the incense. It is carried by the thurifer or by another server.

BOBECHE: A disk or "collar" of metal, glass, plastic, or paper used to catch the wax dripping down a candle.

BOOK OF THE GOSPELS: Ritual book containing the readings of the Gospel for Sundays, solemnities, feasts of the Lord, and some other occasions. It is carried in procession, and it is placed upon the altar after the Entrance Procession and remains on the altar until the proclamation of the Gospel.

CASSOCK: A long garment, usually black, which buttons or snaps down the front, worn with a surplice.

CHALICE: A cup used to hold the Precious Blood during Mass.

CHASUBLE: The priestly vestment worn only for the celebration of Mass.

CIBORIUM: A covered vessel used to hold consecrated hosts/bread.

CINCTURE: A belt, usually white, which is sometimes used with an alb.

COPE: A cape-like vestment worn by a priest or deacon for liturgies outside Mass, like the Liturgy of the Hours; also worn for processions on Palm Sunday and the Most Holy Body and Blood of Christ.

CORPORAL: A square, white cloth, which is placed over the altar cloth, on which the chalice and paten are placed at the Preparation of the Altar and of the Gifts.

CREDENCE TABLE: A table, usually located in the sanctuary, where the vessels and other necessary items are placed for the celebration of Mass.

CROSIER: A staff carried by the Bishop of a diocese in procession; it usually resembles a shepherd's staff.

CRUCIFER: Server carrying the processional cross. Also called a cross-bearer.

CRUET: A small pitcher made from glass or pottery used to hold the wine or water.

DALMATIC: A vestment that may be worn by the deacon for the celebration of Mass.

EXPOSITION: The rite in which the Blessed Sacrament is "exposed" in a monstrance.

EXTRAORDINARY MINISTER OF HOLY COMMUNION: A non-ordained person who is commissioned to distribute the Body and Blood of Christ for either a single or multiple occasion(s).*

FEAST: Second ranking of liturgical observances of the Lord and of the saints. These days are confined only to the natural day; that is, they do not have a vigil and do not begin the evening before. *See also memorial and solemnity.**

FINGER TOWEL: Towel used to dry the presider's hands.

FONT: A vessel containing holy water, used for the celebration of the sacrament of Baptism. There can be other fonts with holy water located adjacent to the doors of the church.

FRONTAL: A cloth that hangs down the front of an altar, often in the liturgical color, also known as an antependium.

GENUFLECT: An act of reverence—the lowering of one knee to the ground in front of the tabernacle.

GREMIALE: A cloth spread over the lap of the Bishop to protect his vestments during anointing.

HUMERAL VEIL: A cloth placed around the shoulders of a priest or deacon when he carries the Blessed Sacrament, whether in procession or for benediction of the Blessed Sacrament.

INSTITUTED ACOLYTE: A ministry of service to assist at the altar primarily by preparing the altar and sacred vessels for Mass. The acolyte may carry the cross in procession, present the book to and assist the priest or deacon in the Preparation of the Altar and of the Gifts and throughout Mass as needed, serve as an Extraordinary Minister of Holy Communion if necessary, and assist with the purification of sacred vessels. The instituted acolyte may only be male. Although this ministry may exist on its own, it usually is a ministry that a candidate receives prior to his admission to the clerical state (ordination).*

LAVABO: A pitcher and basin used for the washing of the priest's hands during Mass.

LECTIONARY: One of the indispensable liturgical books of Mass containing the readings for Sundays, weekdays, ritual Masses, and votive Masses.

LITURGY: From the Greek *leitourgia*, originally meaning "a public act" (the "work of the people") performed for the good of the community. In the Roman Catholic Church, the word is used in reference to any of the official rites of the Church as found in the Roman ritual book. This would include, for example, Mass, the Liturgy of the Hours, Word services, and celebrations of the sacraments.*

LITURGY OF THE EUCHARIST: Begins with the Preparation of the Gifts and includes the Eucharistic Prayer, Communion Rite, and Prayer after Communion, during which the action of Mass is centered around the altar.*

LITURGY OF THE HOURS: Called "the prayer of the Church," the primary offices of the Liturgy of the Hours are Morning Prayer and Evening

Prayer. It consists largely of the chanting or recitation of psalms. It is prayed daily.

LITURGY OF THE WORD: The part of Mass from the First Reading through the Prayer of the Faithful during which the action of Mass is centered around the ambo.*

LUCERNARIUM: A ceremonial lighting of candles, which sometimes takes place as part of the Office of Evening Prayer in the Liturgy of the Hours.

LUNETTE: Circular or semicircular receptacle placed in the monstrance to hold the Blessed Sacrament visibly for exposition and benediction. It often resembles a crescent moon, hence its name.

MEMORIAL: The third ranking of celebrations of the saints. They are either obligatory (that is, they must be celebrated) or optional. *See also feast and solemnity.**

MITER: The pointed hat worn by a Bishop during celebrations of the liturgy.

MONSTRANCE: A transparent vessel in which a consecrated host is placed so as to be seen by the faithful.

NAVE: The main body of a church, so called from its imagined resemblance to a ship.

OFFERTORY TABLE: A small table, usually located in the nave, where the gifts of bread and wine are placed to be brought forward in procession by members of the assembly.

ORANS: An open-armed gesture for prayer that the ordained assume.

ORDO: A book or leaflet, published locally or regionally, giving detailed information about each day of the liturgical year.

OSTENSORIUM: Another name for a monstrance (see above).

PALL: At funerals, a large cloth, usually white, which is placed over the casket as a reminder of Baptism. *Pall* is also the name for a square of fabric sometimes used to cover the chalice and paten on the credence table before the liturgy.

PASCHAL CANDLE: A large wax candle placed in a tall holder to symbolize the light of the risen Christ. It is blessed at the Easter Vigil on Holy Saturday night. During the Easter season, it is placed near the ambo. It stays there until the end of Pentecost. After Pentecost, it is placed near the Baptismal pool and is used during Baptisms and funerals.

PATEN: A small plate used by the priest to hold the hosts. Ciboria (see above) are generally used for distribution of Holy Communion.

PRIEST CELEBRANT: The priest who officiates or is the primary prayer leader for Mass.

PRESIDENTIAL CHAIR: The chair from where the priest celebrant presides.

PURIFICATOR: A small cloth, usually white, used to wipe the rim of the cup during the Communion Rite at Mass.

PYX: A small container, usually metal, used for holding consecrated hosts.

RELIQUARY: A sacred container displaying relics of the saints.

RITUAL: The word *ritual* comes from the Latin *ritualis* meaning "rite" or "form." Ritual can be described as the prescribed words and actions of a liturgical function.*

RITUAL BOOKS: Official text for Roman Catholic worship. Liturgical or ritual books include the *praenotanda* (pastoral introduction to the rite) and the ritual text with rubrics (directions). The original text is in Latin but is translated into the vernacular.*

ROMAN MISSAL: One of the most important liturgical books used during Mass, containing most of the prayers the priest will need.

RUBRIC: The directions for how to celebrate particular rituals. They are usually noted in ritual books in red (the Latin root of the word).

SACRAMENTARY: *See Roman Missal.*

SACRARIUM: A special sink installed in a sacristy for the cleaning of sacred vessels. It drains directly into the earth, not into the sewer.

SANCTUARY: That area of the church building that contains the altar, ambo, and presidential chair.

SANCTUARY LAMP: A candle or oil lamp that both indicates and gives honor to the presence of the Blessed Sacrament in the tabernacle of a church building.

SERVICE: "Generally speaking this would define the obligation the persons have as creatures toward God to show proper homage and pertains to those acts of the virtue of religion by which they serve God personally and socially."[1]

SOLEMNITY: The highest rank of a liturgical observance. These celebrations include not only the day itself, but also the evening before, beginning with either Evening Prayer or with a vigil Mass. *See also feast and memorial.**

STOLE: A narrow strip of fabric worn by ordained ministers, along with liturgical vestments. Priests wear the stole around the neck, hanging down in front. Deacons wear it over the left shoulder, across the chest, and pinned at the right side.

SURPLICE: A short white garment worn over a cassock.

TABERNACLE: A large, permanent container for the consecrated hosts, reserved in a church building.

TAPER: A long wax-coated wick used to light candles.

THURIBLE: A vessel for carrying incense in procession. It is usually made of metal and hangs from a chain.

THURIFER: The minister who carries the thurible or censer in procession.

TRANSEPTS: The "arms" or sections off the nave in a cruciform-shaped church.

VESTMENTS: The special garments worn by the ministers of the liturgy.

VIMPA: A cloth placed around the shoulders of a server. It is used to hold the miter and crosier when the Bishop is present.

ZUCCHETTO: A skullcap worn by Bishops and others: white for the Pope, red for cardinals, purple for Bishops and Archbishops, and black for abbots.[2]

NOTES

1. Lang, Jovian O., OFM. *Dictionary of the Liturgy.* New York: Catholic Book Publishing, 1989, p. 582.

2. The majority of this glossary has been written by Corinna Laughlin and Robert D. Shadduck. Other definitions (*) are adapted from those provided in other books included in *The Liturgical Ministry Series* (LTP, 2007, 2008).

Acknowledgments

Excerpts from the *New American Bible with Revised New Testament* © 1986, 1970 Confraternity of Christian Doctrine, Inc., Washington, DC. Used with permission. All rights reserved. No portion of the *New American Bible* may be reprinted without permission in writing from the copyright holder.

Excerpts from *Book of Blessings* Copyright © 1988 United States Conference of Catholic Bishops, Washington, DC. Used with permission. All rights reserved. No part of this work may be reproduced or transmitted in any form without the permission in writing from the copyright holder.

Excerpts from the *Lectionary for Mass for Use in the Dioceses of the United States of America*, second typical edition © 1998, 1997, 1970, Confraternity of Christian Doctrine, Inc., Washington, DC. Used with permission. All rights reserved. No portion of this text may be reproduced by any means without permission in writing from the copyright owner.

English translation of the *Catechism of the Catholic Church* for the United States of America Copyright © 1994, United States Catholic Conference, Inc.—Libreria Editrice Vaticana. English translation of the: *Catechism of the Catholic Church Modifications* from the Editio Typica Copyright © 1997, United States Conference, Inc.—Libreria Editrice Vaticana. Used with permission.

Psalm 135:1b–3 is from Lectionary #382, Year I.

Excerpts from *Built of Living Stones* © 2000 United States Conference of Catholic Bishops, Washington, DC. Used with permission. All rights reserved. No part of this work may be reproduced or transmitted in any from without the permission in writing from the copyright holder.

Excerpts from the English translation of *Rite of Baptism for Children* © 1969, International Committee on English in the Liturgy, Inc. (ICEL); excerpts from the English translation of *The Liturgy of the Hours* © 1974, ICEL; excerpts from the English translation of *The Roman Missal* © 1973, ICEL; excerpts from the English translation of *Rite of Penance* © 1974, ICEL; excerpts from the English translation of *Dedication of a Church and an Altar* © 1978, 1989, ICEL; excerpts from the English translation of the "General Norms for the Liturgical Year and Calendar" from *Documents on the Liturgy, 1963–1979: Conciliar, Papal, and Curial Texts* © 1982, ICEL; excerpts from the English translation of *Ceremonial of Bishops* © 1989, ICEL; excerpts from the English translation of *The General Instruction of the Roman Missal* © 2002, ICEL. All rights reserved.

Canticle of Simeon (Nunc Dimittis)

Lord, now you let your servant go in peace;
your Word has been fulfilled:

my own eyes have seen the salvation
which you have prepared in the sight of every people:

a light to reveal you to the nations
and the glory of your people Israel.

I should memorize to

Notes
To <u>Self</u>

Do not panic. I know what I'm doing. It is not like they're going to bite me, and the priest will help. I just can't remember when to go down to get ready to kneel hmmm.

Notes

Notes

Notes
